*Comparing the Works of Calvin
with the Word of God*

T.U.L.I.P.
and the Bible

Dave Hunt

BEND • OREGON

T.U.L.I.P. AND THE BIBLE
Comparing the Works of Calvin with the Word of God

Published by The Berean Call
Copyright ©2012

ISBN 978-1-928660-75-0

Unless otherwise indicated, Scripture quotations are from
The Holy Bible, King James Version (KJV)

The Berean Call
PO Box 7019
Bend, Oregon, 97708-7020

PRINTED IN THE UNITED STATES OF AMERICA

Contents

Introduction

DISCUSSIONS WITH NUMBERS OF PEOPLE around the world reveal that many sincere, Bible-believing Christians are "Calvinists" only by default. Thinking that the only choice is between Calvinism (with its presumed doctrine of eternal security) and Arminianism (with its teaching that salvation can be lost), and confident of Christ's promise to keep eternally those who believe in Him, they therefore consider themselves to be Calvinists.

It takes only a few simple questions to discover that most Christians are largely unaware of what John Calvin and his early followers of the sixteenth and seventeenth centuries actually believed and practiced. Nor do they fully understand what most of today's leading Calvinists believe.

Although there are disputed variations of the Calvinist doctrine, among its chief proponents (whom we quote extensively in context) there is general agreement on certain core beliefs. Many evangelicals who think they are Calvinists will be surprised to learn of Calvin's belief in salvation through infant baptism—and of his grossly un-Christian behavior, at times, as the "Protestant Pope" of Geneva, Switzerland (as documented in *What Love Is This?* and *Calvin's Tyrannical Kingdom*).

Most shocking of all, however, is Calvinism's misrepresentation of God who "is love." It is our prayer that the following pages will enable readers to examine more carefully the vital issues involved—and to follow God's Holy Word and not man.

—*Dave Hunt*

Who Can Understand the Gospel?

CALVINISTS EMPHASIZE that their theology rests upon solid biblical exegesis, being "firmly based...upon the Word of God."[1] Some have gone so far as to assert that "this teaching was held to be the truth by the apostles,"[2] and even that "Christ taught the doctrines that have come to be known as the five points of Calvinism."[3]

According to the Bible itself, however, no one should accept such claims without verifying them from Scripture. Any doctrine claiming to be based on the Bible must be carefully checked against the Bible—an option open to anyone who knows God's Word. Relying upon one supposed biblical expert for an evaluation of the opinions of another would be going in circles. No matter whose opinion one accepted, the end result would be the same: one would still be held hostage to human opinion. Each individual must personally check out all opinions directly from the Bible. Yet I was being advised to keep silent on the basis that only those with special qualifications were competent to check Calvinism against the Bible, an idea that in itself contradicted Scripture.

The inhabitants of the city of Berea, though not even Christians when Paul first preached the gospel to them, "searched the scriptures daily, [to see] whether those things [Paul preached] were so" (Acts 17:11)—and they were commended as "noble" for doing so. Yet leading Calvinists insist that it requires special (and apparently lengthy) preparation for anyone to become qualified to examine that peculiar doctrine in light of the Bible. Why?

After all, the Bible itself declares that a "young man" can understand its instructions and thereby "cleanse his way" (Psalm 119:9). Even a child can know the Holy Scriptures through home instruction from a mother and grandmother (2 Timothy 1:5; 3:15). Timothy was certainly not a seminary-trained theologian, yet Paul considered him competent to study and "rightly divide" God's Word. If special expertise were required to test Calvinism against Scripture, that would be proof enough that this peculiar doctrine did not come from valid biblical exegesis. Anything that enigmatic, by very definition, could not have been derived from the Bible, which itself claims to be written for the simple:

> For ye see your calling, brethren, how that not many wise men after the flesh, not many mighty, not many noble, are called: but God hath chosen the foolish things of the world to confound the wise; and God

hath chosen the weak things of the world to confound
the things which are mighty.... That no flesh should
glory in his presence. (1 Corinthians 1:26–29)

Should Calvinism Remain a Mystery for the Common Christian?

Many friends, whose obvious sincerity was appreciated, were
telling me that in spite of my quoting John Calvin directly
from his writings, along with quoting leading Calvinists of
today, I was still likely to misrepresent Calvinism. Even after
many hours of detailed discussion with Calvinist friends, they
still told me, "You just don't understand Calvinism." Then what
of the claim that Calvinism *is* the gospel and true Christianity?
Could multitudes of mature and fruitful evangelicals have
somehow misunderstood the gospel and Christianity?

Should Calvinism remain a mystery for the common
Christian? That very fact, if true, would be additional proof
that Calvinism was not derived from the Scriptures. How
could something so complicated possibly come from that
upon which every person is capable of meditating day and
night (Psalm 1:1–2), and joyfully received—even by a "little
child"?

But Jesus called them unto him, and said, Suffer
little children to come unto me, and forbid them
not: for of such is the kingdom of God. Verily I say
unto you, Whosoever shall not receive the kingdom
of God as a little child shall in no wise enter therein.
(Luke 18:16-17)

If the essential nourishment God's Word provides is to be every man's daily sustenance for spiritual life (Deuteronomy 8:3), could Calvinism really be *the* biblical gospel and biblical Christianity—and yet be so difficult for the ordinary Christian to understand?

Why should Calvinism be such a complex and apparently esoteric subject that it would require years to comprehend? Such an attitude could very well intimidate many into accepting this belief simply because such a vast array of highly respected theologians and evangelical leaders espouse it. Surely the great majority of Calvinists are ordinary Christians. On what basis, then, without the expertise and intense study that I apparently lacked, were they able to understand and accept it?

As for familiarizing oneself with Calvinism, there are surely more than sufficient resources accessible to anyone genuinely interested in consulting them. Numerous books on that subject are available, both pro and con. *The five points of calvinism* by Edwin H. Palmer, along with books by R. C. Sproul, John Piper, John MacArthur, A. W. Pink, C. H. Spurgeon, and others, are highly recommended by leading Calvinists. Calvin's *Institutes of the Christian Religion,* as well as other of his writings and those of Augustine and John Knox, and other classics, are also readily available. On the other side, the books by Samuel Fisk are informative. Laurence M. Vance's *The Other Side of Calvinism* is an exhaustive treatment of more than 700 pages, with hundreds of footnotes documenting his quotations.

Making Certain of Accuracy and Fairness

To make certain that no mistaken interpretations of the doctrines under consideration survived in this book, a preliminary manuscript was submitted to a number of Calvinist friends and acquaintances for their critiques. Reading and discussing with them their valuable comments, for which I am deeply grateful, has been an education in itself. In that process, it became clearer than ever that Calvinists don't agree on everything even among themselves.

A number of critics have faulted me for not accepting the "corrections" offered by Calvinists, which they, of course, consider necessarily to be true. On the contrary, I have carefully considered (though not accepted) every suggestion—even though Calvinists often contradict each other (and even Calvin himself), and some accuse others of being "hyper-Calvinists." We must each arrive at our own conclusions—and this book is about the serious differences many of us have with Calvinists over the interpretation of key passages of Scripture.

Most Calvinists (but not all) agree upon five major points. Some insist that there are ten or even more relevant points. Palmer suggests, "Calvinism is not restricted to five points: it has thousands of points."[4] It's not likely that we can cover all those alleged points in these pages! Palmer himself deals with only five.

There are a number of disagreements between "five-point" and "four-point" Calvinists. For example, Lewis Sperry Chafer, founder of Dallas Theological Seminary, called himself a "four-point" Calvinist because he rejected Limited Atonement.[5] Vance points out that "Many Baptists in the General Association of

Regular Baptist Churches are four-point Calvinists."[6] To deny one point while accepting the other four, however, has been called by five-point Calvinists the "blessed inconsistency." They are correct. We shall see that each point is a logical consequence of those preceding it. It is not possible to be a Calvinist and hold *logically* and consistently to less than all five points.

We therefore agree with the widely declared statement that one "must hold all five points of Calvinism"[7] because "The Five Points of Calvinism all tie together. He who accepts one of the points will accept the other points."[8] Even those who agree on all five, however, have different ways of understanding and defending them.

Obviously, we cannot cover every variety of opinion in this book but must stick to what the majority would accept as a fair presentation of their beliefs. Some Calvinists accuse others of being hyper-Calvinistic, a label that is difficult to define. We will endeavor to establish the major Calvinist beliefs as clearly as we can.

In the further interest of accuracy, we quote extensively not only Calvin himself but from the writings of numerous Calvinists who are highly regarded by their colleagues. One book from which we quote a number of times is *The Potter's Freedom* by apologist James R. White, which is endorsed by a number of today's evangelical leaders. It is an especially valuable resource because it was written specifically to answer Norman Geisler's objections to certain points of Calvinism raised in his recent book, *Chosen But Free*. There should be more than sufficient citations from authoritative sources for the reader who is willing to go to these references to make absolutely certain that Calvinism is being fairly presented.

An Appeal for Open Discussion

God's foreknowledge, predestination/election, human choice, God's sovereignty, and man's responsibility are widely alleged to be mysteries beyond our ability to reconcile. Therefore, some insist that these concepts should be accepted without any attempt at understanding or reconciling apparent conflicts. The illustration is used repeatedly that as we approach heaven's gate we see written above it, "Whosoever will may come," but once we have entered we see from the inside the words, "Chosen in Him before the foundation of the world." We respect the many church leaders who continue to offer such an explanation as though that were sufficient. There are, however, several compelling reasons for not acquiescing to that popular position.

First of all, God intends for us to understand His Word rather than to plead "mystery" over vital portions of it. He has given it for our learning. Of God's Word the psalmist said, "it is a lamp unto my feet, and a light unto my path" (Psalms 119:105), and such it is intended to be for each of us today. Peter acknowledged that there are "things hard to be understood" and warned that Scripture is sometimes twisted by some, resulting in destruction to those who do so (2 Peter 3:16). God never suggests, however, that there is any part of His Word that we should not attempt to understand fully. Inasmuch as many passages in Scripture are devoted to the difficult themes we will address, we can confidently expect that the Bible itself will clarify the issues.

Second, the history of the church from its earliest beginnings has involved sharp differences of opinion on many vital subjects, including the gospel itself. Numerous destructive heresies have developed and have been vigorously opposed. Neither Christ nor His apostles considered divergent views on the essentials of the gospel to be normal or acceptable, but commanded the believers to "earnestly contend for the faith which was once delivered to the saints" (Jude 3). That command applies to us today.

Third, it hardly seems that our Lord would have us draw back from seriously considering and understanding foreknowledge and election/predestination, as well as man's responsibility and how it all fits together in God's sovereign grace. Although we may never see the entire body of Christ in perfect agreement, each of us is responsible to understand these issues as clearly as each one is able, through diligent study—and to help one another in the process.

Finally, God calls upon us to seek Him in order that we may know Him, though His ways and His thoughts are as far above ours as "the heavens are higher than the earth" (Isaiah 55:8–9). Surely, as we come to know God better, we will understand His Word and His will more fully. God is our Savior; to know Him is life eternal (John 17:3). Knowing God must include a deepening understanding of all He has revealed to us in His Word.

We are to live, as Christ said (quoting His own declaration as the *I AM* to Israel through Moses in Deuteronomy 8:3), not "by bread alone, but by *every* word that proceedeth out of the mouth of God" (Matthew 4:4). Solomon said, "*Every* word of God is pure" (Proverbs 30:5; emphases added).

Then we must carefully consider and seek to understand *every word*.

The Most Compelling Reason

It is a general assumption that, whatever other disagreements we may have, when it comes to the gospel of our salvation both Calvinists and non-Calvinists are in full agreement. Some Calvinists, however, disagree, claiming (as we have already seen) that the biblical gospel *is Calvinism*. For example: "God's plan of salvation revealed in the Scriptures consists of what is popularly known as the Five Points of Calvinism."[9] Loraine Boettner declares, "The great advantage of the Reformed Faith is that in the framework of the Five Points of Calvinism it sets forth clearly what the Bible teaches concerning the way of salvation."[10] Others insist that "if you do not know the Five Points of Calvinism, you do not know the gospel, but some perversion of it...."[11] B. B. Warfield claimed, "Calvinism is evangelicalism in its purest and only stable expression."[12]

Such claims that the Five Points alone constitute the gospel raise concerns about Calvinism to a new level! If much special study is required to understand Calvinism, and if years of Bible study still leave one ignorant on this subject, and if Calvinism *is the gospel of our salvation*—then where does that leave the multitudes who think they are saved but are ignorant of Calvinism? This question may seem divisive but it cannot be ignored.

Another grave question is raised concerning the proclamation of the gospel to the whole world as Christ commanded. Calvinists insist that their doctrine does not diminish the zeal with which the gospel is to be preached. To support this assertion, they name some of the great preachers and missionaries who were staunch Calvinists, such as George Whitefield,

Adoniram Judson, William Carey, and others. And it is true that, although they know that many to whom they preach are not among the elect, some Calvinists nevertheless preach earnestly so that the elect may hear and believe.

Certainly, however, the zeal of such men and women in bringing the gospel to the world could not be *because* of their Calvinism but only *in spite* of it. To believe that those who will be saved have been predestined to salvation by God's decree, that no others can be saved, and that the elect must be regenerated by God's sovereign act without the gospel or any persuasion by any preacher, or by any faith in God on their part, could hardly provide motivation for earnestly preaching the gospel. No matter how the Calvinist tries to argue to the contrary, such a belief can only lessen the zeal a reasonable person might otherwise have, to reach the lost with the gospel of God's grace in Christ.

Facing a Real Dilemma

The gospel that Peter and Paul and the other apostles preached was for everyone in the audiences they faced, wherever they went. It was not a message that only the elect could believe. Peter told Cornelius and his family and friends, "And he [Christ] commanded us to preach unto the people [not to a select group]...that whosoever [among the people to whom He preached] believeth in him shall receive remission of sins" (Acts 10:42–43).

In contrast, Calvin's gospel says that Christ died, and His blood atones, for only the elect. Could this be the same gospel Paul preached? Paul proclaimed to audiences, "We declare unto [all of] you glad tidings..." (Acts 13:32). The "glad tidings" of the gospel that Paul preached echoed what the angel of the Lord had said to the shepherds at the time of Christ's birth: "I bring you tidings of great joy, which shall be to all people..." (Luke 2:10). These tidings of great joy concerned the fact that "the Savior of the world" (Luke 2:11; John 4:42) had been born.

Calvin's gospel, however, says that Christ is not the Savior of the world but only of the elect. How could that message be "tidings of great joy" to those whom the Savior did not come to save and for whose sins He refused to die?

Paul could and did honestly say to everyone he met, "Christ died for you." In complete contrast, a book on biblical counseling that we have long recommended to readers declares, "As a reformed Christian, the writer [author] believes that counselors must not tell any unsaved counselee that Christ died for him, for *they cannot say that.* No man knows except Christ himself who are his elect for whom he died" (emphasis added).[13]

The author calls himself a "*reformed* Christian." What might *that* mean? Obviously, Calvin's message of salvation for a select group *does not* bring "great joy" to "all people."

Palmer writes, "But thank God that Christ's death was an absolute guarantee that every single one of the elect would be saved."[14] So great joy comes to the elect alone! As for the rest, Calvin's doctrine that God had predestined their damnation could hardly be "tidings of great joy"! This is the way Calvin put it:

> To many this seems a perplexing subject, because they deem it most incongruous that of the great body of mankind some should be predestinated to salvation,

> and others to destruction.... From this we infer, that
> all who know not that they are the peculiar people of
> God, must be wretched from perpetual trepidation....[15]

What gospel is this that is cause for joy to only some? It cannot be the biblical gospel that the angels announced! Because of the eternal importance of that question for the whole world to whom Christ commanded us to take the gospel, we are compelled to examine Calvinism closely in light of Scripture. Could it really be true, as Arthur C. Custance insists, that "Calvinism is the Gospel and to teach Calvinism is in fact to preach the Gospel"?[16]

Is Calvinism founded upon the plain text of Scripture? Or does it require interpreting common words and phrases such as *all, all men, world, everyone that thirsteth, any man,* and *whosoever will* to mean "the elect"? Is a peculiar interpretation of Scripture required to sustain this doctrine?

Our concern is for the defense of the character of the true God, the God of mercy and love whose "tender mercies are over all his works" (Psalms 145:9). The Bible declares that He is "not willing that any should perish, but that all should come to repentance" (2 Peter 3:9); "who will have all men to be saved, and to come unto the knowledge of the truth" (1 Timothy 2:4). Such is the God of the Bible, from Genesis to Revelation.

Open examination and discussion of important issues—especially the gospel and the very nature and character of God—can only be healthy for the body of Christ. It is my prayer that our investigation of Calvinism and its comparison with God's Holy Word, as expressed in the following pages, will bring helpful and needed clarification.

1. W. J. Seaton, *The Five Points of Calvinism* (Carlisle, PA: The Banner of Truth Trust, 1970), 8.

2. Jimmie B. Davis, *The Berea Baptist Banner*, February 5, 1995, 30.

3. Mark Duncan, *The Five Points of Christian Reconstruction from the Lips of Our Lord* (Edmonton, AB: Still Waters Revival Books, 1990), 10.

4. Edwin H. Palmer, foreword to *the five points of calvinism* (Grand Rapids, MI: Baker Books, enlarged ed., 20th prtg. 1999), 1.

5. Lewis Sperry Chafer, *Systematic Theology* (Dallas, TX: Dallas Seminary Press, 1948), 3:184.

6. Laurence M. Vance, *The Other Side of Calvinism* (Pensacola, FL: Vance Publications, rev. ed. 1999), 147.

7. Charles W. Bronson, *The Extent of the Atonement* (Pasadena, TX: Pilgrim Publications, 1992), 19.

8. Palmer, *five points*, 27.

9. Leonard J. Coppes, *Are Five Points Enough? The Ten Points of Calvinism* (Denver, CO: self-published, 1980), 55.

10. Loraine Boettner, *The Reformed Faith* (Phillipsburg, NJ: Presbyterian and Reformed Publishing Co., 1983), 24.

11. Fred Phelps, "The Five Points of Calvinism" (*The Berea Baptist Banner*, February 5, 1990), 21.

12. Benjamin B. Warfield, *Calvin and Augustine,* ed. Samuel G. Craig (Phillipsburg, NJ: Presbyterian and Reformed Publishing Co., 1956), 497.

13. Jay E. Adams, *Competent to Counsel* (Grand Rapids, MI: Baker Book House, 1970), 70.

14. Palmer, *five points*, 92.

15. John Calvin, *Institutes of the Christian Religion,* trans. Henry Beveridge (Grand Rapids, MI: Wm. Eerdmans Publishing Company, 1998 ed.), III: xxi, 1.

16. Arthur C. Custance, *The Sovereignty of Grace* (Phillipsburg, NJ: Presbyterian and Reformed Publishing Co., 1979), 302.

Confusion, Councils, and Controversy

CALVINISM IS OFTEN contrasted with Arminianism, so named after Jacobus Arminius (1560–1609). All those who do not fully agree with Calvinists on all five points of TULIP (see below) are almost automatically accused of being Arminians (not to be confused with ethnic Armenians), yet many against whom this charge is laid have never heard the term. Moreover, many Calvinists who malign Arminius have never read his works and know nothing more than hearsay about him and his beliefs.

Ironically, this Dutch theologian started out as a Calvinist and even studied under Beza in Calvin's seminary in Geneva. He was a devout follower of Christ and suffered much for his faith. His entire family was murdered in his absence when Spanish Catholic troops enforcing the Inquisition massacred the population of his hometown of Oudewater in Holland.

Arminius was wrongfully charged with nearly every false doctrine ever invented, from Socinianism (denial of predestination, of the true nature of the Atonement and of the Trinity) to Pelagianism (the denial that Adam's sin affected his posterity, an undue emphasis upon free will, salvation by grace plus works, and the possibility of sinless perfection). Thus to be called an Arminian is a more serious charge than many of either the accusers or the accused realize. So strong was Calvinism in certain parts of Europe in Arminius's day that to disagree with it was tantamount to a denial of the gospel and even of God's entire Word—and it could cost one's life. In England, for example, a 1648 Act of Parliament made a rejection of Calvinistic infant baptism punishable by death.[1]

Arminius had to bear the special onus that came upon any Protestant of his day, especially in Holland, who dared to take a second look at Calvinism from the Scriptures, a guilt sometimes attached to non-Calvinists today. He was accused of having secret leanings toward Roman Catholicism, in spite of his open denunciation of Catholic sacraments and of the papacy as the kingdom of Antichrist. Upon visiting Rome to see the Vatican for himself, Arminius reported that he saw "'the mystery of iniquity' in a more foul, ugly, and detestable form than his imagination could ever have conceived."[2] Some of those who have called themselves Arminians promote serious heresy, having "adopted views quite contrary" to what he taught,[3] but Arminius himself was actually biblical in his beliefs and far more Christlike in his life than was Calvin. Vance rightly declares that "Arminius was just as orthodox on the cardinal doctrines of the Christian Faith as any Calvinist, ancient or modern."[4]

Character and Conduct Comparisons

Some Calvinists have criticized the first edition of this book for what they call my alleged "caricature of Calvin [and] adoring portrait of Arminius...." On the contrary, I have simply given the historic facts, which none of my critics have been able to refute. In *Debating Calvinism* (Multnomah, 2004), James White said he would "refute the calumnies [I] launched at... Calvin [and] Augustine." I'm still waiting. It is unconscionable that Calvinists have swept under the rug Calvin's un-Christlike conduct—and have refused to acknowledge the facts when confronted with them.

There is no denying that Calvin was abusive, derisive, contemptuous, insulting, disparaging, harsh, and sarcastic in his writings and opinions expressed of others. Nor was this only in his language but frequently in his actual treatment of many who dared to disagree with him—as we have briefly shown.

In contrast, Arminius was a consistent Christian in his writings and kind and considerate in his treatment of others. Nowhere in his writings or actions does one find anything of the sarcasm, derision, and contempt for contrary opinions that characterize Calvin's writings. There was nothing about Arminius to suggest revenge against one's enemies or the use of violence in the cause of Christ—much less the death sentence for heresy that was enforced in Calvin's Geneva.

In evaluating either of these two strong leaders, one must also remember that, just as the Five Points of Calvinism were not formulated by Calvin but by the Synod of Dort, so neither was it Arminius who articulated the five points of Arminianism, but the Remonstrants who did so after his death.

Arminius and His Teachings

Arminius stood uncompromisingly for sound doctrine and believed in the infallibility and inerrancy of the Bible as inspired by God. He rejected the Mass as a denial of "the truth and excellence of the sacrifice of Christ."[5] He joined in calling the pope "the adulterer and pimp of the Church, the false prophet...the enemy of God...the Antichrist...[6] the man of sin, the son of perdition, that most notorious outlaw[7]...[who] shall be destroyed at the glorious advent of Christ,"[8] and urged all true believers to "engage in... the destruction of Popery, as they would...the kingdom of Antichrist...."[9] And he endeavored to "destroy Popery" by his lucid and powerful preaching of the gospel and sound doctrine from God's Word.

Arminius recognized and rejected the false doctrines of Augustine for what they were. In contrast to Augustine, Arminius also rejected the Apocrypha and authority of tradition. He believed in the eternal Sonship of Christ, co-equal and co-eternal with the Father and the Holy Spirit,[10] that Christ came to this earth as a man,[11] that He was Jehovah of the Old Testament[12] who died for our sins, paying the full penalty by His one sacrifice of Himself on the cross,[13] that He was buried, rose again, and ascended to heaven,[14] that man is hopelessly lost and bound by sin, and that salvation is by grace alone through faith alone in Christ alone.[15]

Arminius preached that salvation was entirely through Christ as a work of grace, which God alone could do in the heart. He categorically denied the false charges made against him of Pelagianism and Socinianism.[16] He also, with these words, defended himself against the false charge that he taught the doctrine of falling away:

> For I never…taught any thing contrary to the word of God, or to the Confession and Catechism of the Belgic Churches. At no period have I ceased to make this avowal, and I repeat it on this occasion….Yet since a sinister report, has for a long time been industriously and extensively circulated about me…and since this unfounded rumor has already operated most injuriously against me, I importunately entreat to be favored with your gracious permission to make an ingenuous and open declaration….
>
> [Articles were circulated] as if they had been my composition: when, in reality…they had neither proceeded from me, nor accorded with my sentiments, and, as well as I could form a judgment they appeared to me to be at variance with the word of God….
>
> Twice I repeated this solemn asseveration, and besought the brethren "not so readily to attach credit to reports that were circulated concerning me, nor so easily to listen to any thing that was represented as proceeding from me or that had been rumored abroad to my manifest injury…."
>
> My sentiments respecting the perseverance of the saints are, that those persons who have been grafted into Christ by true faith, and have thus been made partakers of his life-giving Spirit, possess sufficient powers [or strength] to fight against Satan, sin, the world and their own flesh, and to gain the victory over these enemies— yet not without the assistance of the grace of the same Holy Spirit. Jesus Christ also by his Spirit assists them in all their temptations, and affords them the ready aid of his hand; and, provided they stand prepared for the

battle, implore his help, and be not wanting to themselves, Christ preserves them from falling. So that it is not possible for them, by any of the cunning craftiness or power of Satan, to be either seduced or dragged out of the hands of Christ....

Though I here openly and ingenuously affirm, I never taught that a true believer can, either totally or finally fall away from the faith, and perish; yet I will not conceal, that there are passages of scripture which seem to me to wear this aspect; and those answers to them which I have been permitted to see, are not of such a kind as to approve themselves on all points to my understanding. On the other hand, certain passages are produced for the contrary doctrine [of unconditional perseverance] which are worthy of much consideration....

I am not conscious to myself, of having taught or entertained any other sentiments concerning the justification of man before God, than those which are held unanimously by the Reformed and Protestant Churches, and which are in complete agreement with their expressed opinions...yet my opinion is not so widely different from [Calvin's] as to prevent me from employing the signature of my own hand in subscribing to those things which he has delivered on this subject [of justification], in the third book of his Institutes; this I am prepared to do at any time, and to give them my full approval.... For I am not of the congregation of those who wish to have dominion over the faith of another man, but am only a minister to believers, with the design of promoting in them an increase of knowledge, truth, piety, peace and joy in Jesus Christ our Lord."[17]

Staunch Calvinist R. K. McGregor Wright acknowledges that Arminius solidly affirmed the eternal security of the saints, although that doctrine was "...abandoned by his followers...a few years after his death."[18] Arminius is maligned and denounced today by Calvinists, while Augustine is praised. Even while admitting that Arminius "affirmed dogmatically that it is impossible for believers to decline from salvation," Dillow insists that "Arminius believes salvation can be lost."[19] J. I. Packer quotes with approval "Robert Traill, the Scottish Puritan, [who] wrote in 1692, 'The principles of Arminianism are the natural dictates of a carnal mind, which is enmity both to the law of God, and to the gospel of Christ, and, next to the dead sea of Popery (into which also this stream runs), have, since Pelagius to this day, been the greatest plague of the Church of Christ, and it is likely will be till his second coming.'"[20] Sheldon, however, says, "The doctrinal system of Arminius, who is confessed on all hands to have been a man of most exemplary spirit and life, was the Calvinistic system with no further modification than necessarily resulted from rejecting the tenet of absolute predestination."[21] A leading Arminian of the nineteenth century summarized his understanding of that doctrine:

> Arminianism teaches that God in Jesus Christ made provision fully for the salvation of all those who, by repentance towards God and faith in our Lord Jesus Christ, accept the terms [of the gospel], and all who do thus accept are eternally saved.[22]

One could hardly argue with that statement. Yet Calvinists continue to accuse Arminius of teaching that salvation could be lost—and to label as "Arminians" anyone who disagrees with them. The same is often the case today.

The Break with Calvinism

Arminius was as determined as Calvin to follow only the Lord and His Word. That sincere desire got him into trouble because he considered himself no more "bound to adopt all the private interpretations of the Reformed"[23] than those of the Roman Catholic Church.[24] He concluded from earnest study of the Scriptures that in some respects Calvinism was simply not biblical. And he suffered false accusations and persecution for that careful and prayerful opinion—as do non-Calvinists today.

Arminius was convinced from the Scriptures that those who will be in heaven will be there because they believed the gospel, not because God elected them to be saved, and regenerated them without any faith on their part. He firmly believed and taught predestination as "an eternal and gracious decree of God in Christ, by which He determines to justify and adopt believers, and to endow them with life eternal, but to condemn unbelievers and impenitent persons."[25] What E. H. Broadbent in his classic *The Pilgrim Church* had to say about Arminius stands in stark contrast to the slander the latter still suffers from Calvinists:

> Brought up under the influence of Calvin's teaching, Arminius—acknowledged by all as a man of spotless character, in ability and learning unexcelled—was chosen to write in defense of Calvinism of the less extreme kind, which was felt to be endangered by the attacks

made upon it. Studying the subject, however, he came
to see that much that he held was indefensible; that it
made God the author of sin, set limits to His saving
grace, left the majority of mankind without hope or
possibility of salvation.

He saw from the Scriptures that the atoning work
of Christ was for all, and that man's freedom of choice
is a part of the divine decree. Coming back to the original teaching of Scripture and faith of the Church, he
avoided the extremes into which both parties to the
long controversy had fallen. His statement of what he
had come to believe involved him personally in conflicts
which so affected his spirit as to shorten his life [he died
at the age of 49, Calvin at 55]. His teaching took a vivid
and evangelical form later, in the Methodist revival.[26]

Fisk agrees that "Arminianism comes from the name of a
man who first embraced the Calvinistic system, was called upon
to defend it against the opposition, and who upon further study
came around to a more moderate position."[27] McNeill, himself a Presbyterian, is honest enough to say that Arminius "does
not repudiate predestination, but condemns supralapsarianism
[that God from eternity past predestined the non-elect to sin
and to suffer eternal damnation] as subversive of the gospel."[28]
Earle E. Cairns explains the major differences between the two
systems:

His [Arminius's] attempt to modify Calvinism so
that...God might not be considered the author
of sin, nor man an automaton in the hands of
God, brought down upon him the opposition....
Both Arminius and Calvin taught that man, who

inherited Adam's sin, is under the wrath of God.
But Arminius believed that man was able to initi-
ate his salvation after God had granted him the
primary grace to enable his will to cooperate with
God....[29] Arminius accepted election but believed
that the decree to save some and damn others had
"its foundation in the foreknowledge of God."[30] Thus
election was conditional rather than unconditional....
Arminius also believed that Christ's death was sufficient for all but that it was efficient only for believers.[31]
Calvin limited the atonement to those elected to salvation. Arminius also taught that men might resist the
saving grace of God,[32] whereas Calvin maintained that
grace was irresistible.[33]

The earnest desire of Arminius had simply been to mitigate
Calvinism's extremes. Of Arminius, Newman says, "He was recognized as among the ablest and most learned men of his time.
His expository sermons were so lucid, eloquent, and well delivered as to attract large audiences. He was called upon from time
to time to write against opponents of Calvinism, which he did
in a moderate and satisfactory way. When pestilence was raging
in 1602, he distinguished himself by heroic service."[34]

In the early days, no one lashed out more viciously at
"Arminians" than John Owen, who referred to "the poison
of Arminianism...hewing at the very root of Christianity."[35]
This effort reached its peak in his lengthy treatise against "the
doctrines of Arminius" titled *A Display of Arminianism*, first
published in 1642 by order of the Committee of the House
of Commons in Parliament for the Regulating of Printing and
Publishing of Books. Seemingly lost in the earnest polemics

was one cautionary word in the "Prefatory Note," which went unheeded then as now: "It may be questioned if Owen sufficiently discriminates the doctrine of Arminius from the full development which his system, after his death, received in the hands of his followers."[36]

Arminianism and State Churches

Arminius's moderate view attracted a large following. Many Protestant pastors, uncomfortable with the extremes of Calvinism and with its militancy against those who disagreed, began to preach the same modified Calvinism as Arminius and received considerable opposition from Calvinists. The latter, following Augustine's teaching and the practice of Rome, saw church and state as partners, with the state enforcing sanctions against whomever the church considered to be heretics—an intolerance that Arminius and his followers opposed. McGregor writes that "the entire process of the Reformation took place in the context of state churches, with secular power supporting the Reformers and protecting their gains.[37]

This great error was the legacy of Constantine, the first to forbid anyone outside the established church to meet for religious purposes and the first to confiscate the property of those who did. Believing that baptism was "the salvation of God...the seal which confers immortality...the seal of salvation,"[38] he had waited until just before his death to be baptized so as not to risk sinning thereafter and losing his salvation. Later, Emperor Theodosius issued an edict making "the religion which was taught by St. Peter to the Romans, which has been faithfully preserved by tradition"[39] the official faith of the empire. As noted earlier; adherents were to be called "Catholic Christians," and all others were forbidden to meet in their churches.[40] One historian has explained the tragic effect for the church:

> The Scriptures were now no longer the standard of the Christian faith...[but] the decisions of fathers and councils...religion propagated not by the apostolic methods of persuasion, accompanied with the meekness and gentleness of Christ, but by imperial edicts and decrees; nor were gainsayers to be brought to conviction by...reason and scripture, but persecuted and destroyed.[41]

Such was the official relationship between church and state that Calvin inherited from Augustine, enforced in Geneva, and which the Calvinists, wherever possible, carried on and used to enforce their will upon those who differed with them. In league with princes, kings, and emperors, the Roman Catholic Church had for centuries controlled all of Europe. The Reformation created a new state church across Europe, in competition with Rome, which was either Lutheran or Calvinist. The latter claim the name "Reformed."

The Presbyterian Church in Scotland, the Church of England, and the Dutch Reformed Church, which persecuted the Arminians in Holland, were all Calvinistic state churches. Tragically, they followed Constantine, Augustine, and Calvin in the unbiblical and grandiose ambition of imposing their brand of Christianity upon all, in partnership with the state.

As David Gay points out:

> In the *Institutes* Calvin said that civil government is
> assigned to foster and maintain the external worship
> of God, to defend sound doctrine and the condition
> of the church. He dismissed the Anabaptists as stupid
> fanatics because they argued that these matters are
> the business of the church, not the civil authorities.
> Nevertheless, Calvin was wrong; they were right.... He
> was writing from the viewpoint of Constantine, not
> the New Testament....[42]

Synods, Assemblies, Councils, and Confessions

Those who disagree with Calvinism today on the basis of their
understanding of God's Word are accused of abandoning,
ignoring, or even defying the great confessions and established
creeds of the church. We must ask, "Which church?" Roman
Catholics also refer to "the Church" in a similar manner, but
millions of true believers were not part of it for centuries before
the Reformation, refusing to bow to the popes or to submit to
Rome's heresies. Calvinists today, looking back upon the first
century or so of the Reformation, refer to "the church" in much
the same way, meaning state churches carrying on what Calvin
began in Geneva, with those who disagree looked down upon
as heretics who reject "the Reformed faith"—thus equating
Calvinism with the Reformation.

Calvin diligently persecuted even to the death those
who disagreed with his extreme views on sovereignty and

predestination. Yet he tolerated the many heresies of Augustine—and even adopted some. We find only praise in his writings for this man who held to so much that was unbiblical. In fact, Calvin looked to Augustine as the authority justifying his own erroneous beliefs and practices.

It must be remembered that the Reformation creeds and confessions were formulated not by agreement among all Christians but by either the Lutheran or the Calvinist segment alone. The Synod of Dort and the Westminster Assembly, referred to by Calvinists as authoritative declarations of Christian truth, were dominated by Calvinists and forced Calvinism as the official state religion upon everyone.

So the accusation that one fails to follow these "great Reformed confessions" is merely another way of saying that one disagrees with Calvinism! It also furthers the false impression that Calvinism was the official belief held by all of the Reformers. Concerning the five points of Calvinism, Hodges writes, "None of these ideas has any right to be called normative Protestant theology. None has ever been held by a wide cross-section of Christendom. Most importantly, none of them is biblical...all of them lie outside the proper parameters of Christian orthodoxy."[43]

The Five Arminian Points

Arminius was part of the state Dutch Reformed Church, as were the leaders who carried on his beliefs after his premature death in 1609. Inevitably, open controversy developed over predestination and whether the Belgic Confession and Heidelberg Catechism should be reviewed for possible revision.

To discuss the issues, forty-six Arminian ministers met privately in Gouda, Holland, on January 14, 1610. They drew up and signed a Remonstrance (protest) against Calvinism, stating that its doctrines were "not contained in the Word of God nor in the Heidelberg Catechism, and are unedifying—yea, dangerous— and should not be preached to Christian people."[44]

The Remonstrance comprised five brief paragraphs that became known as the five points of Arminianism. In summary they stated:

1. That God from eternity past determined to save all who believe in Jesus and to "leave the incorrigible and unbelieving in sin and under wrath...."

2. That Christ died for and obtained redemption and forgiveness of sins for all, but these benefits are effective only for those who believe on Christ.

3. That man cannot "think, will or do anything that is truly good," and that includes "saving faith," but must be regenerated.

4. That God's grace is absolutely essential for salvation, but that it may be resisted.

5. That those truly saved through faith in Christ are empowered by the Holy Spirit to resist sin; but whether they could fall away from the faith "must be more particularly determined out of the Holy Scripture, before we ourselves can teach it with full persuasion of our minds."

The Calvinist response came a few months later in the form of a Counter-Remonstrance, which contained seven articles. The second and third points have been combined under the heading of Unconditional Election, with the sixth and seventh points combined under Perseverance of the Saints, resulting in what has become known as the Five Points of Calvinism.

Vance summarizes this declaration well as follows:

1. Because the whole race has fallen in Adam and become corrupt and powerless to believe, God draws out of condemnation those whom he has chosen unto salvation, passing by the others.

2. The children of believers, as long as they do not manifest the contrary, are to be reckoned among God's elect.

3. God has decreed to bestow faith and perseverance and thus save those whom he has chosen to salvation.

4. God delivered up his Son Jesus Christ to die on the cross to save only the elect.

5. The Holy Spirit, externally through the preaching of the Gospel, works a special grace internally in the hearts of the elect, giving them power to believe.

6. Those whom God has decreed to save are supported and preserved by the Holy Spirit so that they cannot finally lose their true faith.

7. True believers do not carelessly pursue the lusts of the flesh, but work out their own salvation in the fear of the Lord.[45]

The Growing Controversy

The Counter-Remonstrance was in turn answered by The Opinion of the Remonstrants. This was a far more lengthy document which went into great detail to establish what the Remonstrants "in conscience have thus far considered and still consider to be in harmony with the Word of God...." It contained lengthy objections to Calvinism under four headings, the main points of which are summarized in the following excerpts:

From Section I (10 paragraphs):

3. God...has not ordained the fall...has not deprived Adam of the necessary and sufficient grace, does also not...bring some [men] unto [eternal] life, but deprive others of the benefit of life....

4. God has not decreed without intervening actual sins to leave by far the greater part of men, excluded from all hope of salvation, in the fall.

5. God has ordained that Christ should be the atonement for the sins of the whole world, and by virtue of this decree He has decided to justify and to save those who believe in Him, and to provide men with the means necessary and sufficient unto faith...

6. No one is rejected from eternal life nor from the means sufficient thereto by any antecedent absolute decree....

From Section II (4 paragraphs):

1. The price of salvation, which Christ offered to God...paid for all and every man, according to... the grace of God the Father; and therefore no one is definitely excluded from...the benefits of the death of Christ by an absolute and antecedent decree of God.

3. Although Christ has merited reconciliation with God and the forgiveness of sins for all men...no one becomes an actual partaker of the benefits of the death of Christ except by faith....

From Section III (12 paragraphs):

5. The efficacious grace by which anyone is converted is not irresistible, and although God through the Word and the inner operation of His Spirit so influences the will that He both bestows the power to believe and...indeed causes man to believe, nevertheless man is able of himself to despise this grace, not to believe, and thus to perish through his own fault.

6. Although according to the altogether free will of God the disparity of divine grace may be very great, nevertheless the Holy Spirit bestows, or is ready to bestow, as much grace upon all men and every man to whom God's Word is preached as is sufficient for the furtherance of the sufficient grace unto faith and conversion whom God is said to be willing to save according to the decree of absolute election, but also they who are not actually converted.

12. We also hold to be false and horrible that God should in a hidden manner incite men to the sin which He openly forbids; that those who sin do not act contrary to the true will of God…that it is according to justice a crime worthy of death to do God's will.

From Section IV (8 paragraphs):

3. True believers can fall from true faith and fall into such sins as cannot be consistent with true and justifying faith, and not only can this happen, but it also not infrequently occurs.

4. True believers can through their own fault…finally fall away and go lost.

5. Nevertheless we do not believe, though true believers sometimes fall into grave and conscience-devastating sins, that they immediately fall from all hope of conversion, but we acknowledge that it can happen that God according to His abundant mercy, again calls them to conversion through His grace….

6. Therefore we heartily reject the following doctrines, which are daily spread abroad among the people in public writings, as being harmful to piety and good morals; namely: 1) That true believers cannot sin deliberately, but only out of ignorance and weakness. 2) That true believers through no sins can fall from the grace of God. 3) That a thousand sins, yea, all the sins of the whole world, cannot render election invalid; when it is added to

this that all men are obligated to believe that they
are chosen unto salvation, and therefore cannot fall
from election, we present for consideration what a
wide door that opens for carnal certainty. 4) That
to believers and to the elect no sins, however great
and grave they may be, are imputed....5) That true
believers, having fallen into corrupt heresies, into
grave and shameful sins, such as adultery and murder, on account of which the Church, according
to the institution of Christ, is obligated to testify
that she cannot tolerate them in her external fel-
lowship, and that they shall have no part in the
kingdom of Christ, unless they repent, nevertheless cannot totally and finally fall from the faith.

8. A true believer can and must be certain for the
future that he, granted intervening, watching,
praying, and other holy exercises, can persevere
in the true faith, and that the grace of God to
persevere will never be lacking to him; but we do
not see how he may be assured that he will never
neglect his duty in the future, but in the works of
faith, piety and love, as befits a believer, persevere
in this school of Christian warfare. Neither do we
deem it necessary that the believer should be certain of this.[46]

These four headings (which clearly departed from what
Arminius had taught) were understood to contain five points,
which the Calvinists at the Synod of Dort answered with what
has become known as the Five Points of Calvinism. The major
difference is obvious: the Arminians put the blame for man's
eternal punishment upon man himself for rejecting the gospel

by his own free will, though he could have accepted it through God's gracious enabling; whereas the Calvinists laid sin itself and the damnation of man totally upon God, who simply predestined everything to turn out that way. A. W. Tozer, respected by many Calvinists, declared, "So when man exercises his freedom [of choice], he is fulfilling the sovereignty of God, not canceling it out."[47]

The State of the Netherlands, in its concern for unity among its citizens, ordered both parties to meet to iron out their differences. Six leaders from each side met in the Hague on March 31, 1611, but failed to reach an agreement. While the Arminians pleaded for tolerance, the Calvinists were determined to convene a national conference to have their opponents declared heretics. Of course, the view at that time was that the state would exact the prescribed penalties upon heretics, up to and including death.

The Great Synod of Dort (Dordrecht)

The persisting theological differences eventually involved the government in an internal battle between political rivals. The Calvinists won out, Prince Maurice siding with them. Magistrates sympathetic to the Arminians were replaced. This later paved the way for the national synod, which, after letters sent inviting foreign representatives, was then convened at Dordrecht on November 13, 1618, and lasted into May of the following year.

Convinced that they were standing for truth, each Calvinist delegate took an oath to follow only the Word of God and to "aim at the glory of God, the peace of the Church, and especially the preservation of the purity of doctrine. So help me, my Savior, Jesus Christ! I beseech him to assist me by his Holy Spirit."[48]

Calvinists ever since have hailed Dort as a gathering of history's most godly leaders, who sincerely followed their oath. In John Wesley's opinion, however, Dort was as impartial as the Council of Trent.[49] In fact, Dort had been called by state officials favoring the Calvinists for the sole purpose of supporting the Calvinists and condemning the Arminians, so it can hardly be considered an impartial tribunal, and certainly did not represent a consensus among true believers.

Moreover, Baptists who today point to Dort as the articulation of what they believe are, as Vance points out,[50] "not only conforming to a Dutch Reformed State-Church creed, they are following Augustine, for as the Reformed theologian Herman Hanko asserts, 'Our fathers at Dordrecht knew well that these truths set forth in the Canons could not only be traced back to the Calvin Reformation; they could be traced back to the theology of St. Augustine.... For it was Augustine who had originally defined these truths.'[51] Custance insists that the Five Points were 'formulated implicitly by Augustine.'"[52]

The Arminians were not allowed to plead their case as equals, but were removed from the status of delegates to that of defendants, and were summarily expelled from the synod and publicly denounced. After Dort, the Remonstrants were asked to recant or be banished. More than 200 Arminian ministers were removed from their pulpits and many were exiled. There was an attempt to establish a harsh Calvinistic theocracy where only Calvinism could be publicly proclaimed, but it lasted only a short time. It was not, however, until 1625 that persecution of Arminians officially ceased.[53]

Cairns calls the Great Synod of Dort "an international Calvinistic assembly" in which the Arminians "came before the meeting in the role of defendants." Calvinists have called Dort "a symbol of the triumph of orthodox Calvinism in the Netherlands."[54] Louis Berkhof declares, "Five thoroughly Calvinistic Canons, in which the doctrines of the Reformation, and particularly of Calvin, on the disputed points are set forth with clearness and precision."[55]

Ever since Dort, Calvinists have hailed these Canons as "a bulwark, a defense, of the truth of God's Word concerning our salvation."[56] We have already quoted a variety of Calvinist leaders, to the effect that Calvinism's Five Points are the gospel. Such opinions should cause concern in the church today in view of the resurgence of Calvinism through the efforts of esteemed evangelical leaders.

Fruits of the Synod of Dort

In evaluating the Synod of Dort and the Five Points of Calvinism that it pronounced, one cannot avoid recognition of the political nature of the gathering. Christ had drawn a clear line of separation between the things that are Caesar's and…"the things that are God's" (Mark 12:17). In tragic contrast, Calvinistic church leaders were acting as instruments of Caesar (the state)—and the state acted on their behalf to punish their opponents. That Calvinists together with the state falsely charged, persecuted, imprisoned, and executed some of the Arminian leaders must also be a consideration in evaluating this entire procedure and its fruits—as well as Calvinism itself.

Although both the Arminians and Calvinists at this time were in agreement as to the church-state alliance, the Arminians had no desire to use the state to enforce their views upon their opponents, but only to protect their own freedom of conscience and practice. Even Calvinists admit that "the divines who composed the Synod of Dort generally held that the civil magistrate was entitled to inflict pains and penalties as a punishment for heresy" and that, in contrast, the Arminians advocated "toleration and forbearance in regard to differences of opinion upon religious subjects." [57]

Consider, for example, the fate of the four main leaders of the Arminian movement. John Uytenbogaert, who had studied at Geneva under Calvin's successor, Beza, and served as chaplain to Prince Maurice (son and successor of William of Orange), was exiled after the Synod of Dort and had his goods confiscated. Simon Episcopius, a professor of theology and chief spokesman for the Arminians at Dort, was banished. John Van Oldenbarnevelt, who was advocate-general of Holland and a national hero for helping William of Orange to negotiate the Union of Utrecht, was falsely charged with treason and was beheaded. Hugo Grotius, a famed lawyer known worldwide for his expertise in international law, was sentenced to life in prison but escaped and later became Swedish ambassador to Paris.

What biblical basis could anyone propose for exacting such penalties for a disagreement over doctrine? If the Calvinists could be so wrong in so much that is so important, might they not also be wrong in some basic theological assumptions? Yet in spite of a complete misunderstanding of and disobedience concerning such vital and fundamental New Testament teachings as separation of church and state (John 15:14–21; 16:33;

1 John 2:15–17) and nonimposition of belief by force, these men are hailed as "great divines" and the doctrine they forcefully imposed on others is embraced as the truth of God—now called "the Reformed faith" and "the doctrines of grace"—to be accepted by all today. The church, once persecuted, now persecuted fellow believers!

The Westminster Assembly

Dort was followed in 1643 by a similar prestigious gathering of "divines" in England. The Westminster Assembly was also under the auspices of the state. The six-year-long Assembly formulated The Westminster Confession of Faith, which has been called "the most systematically complete statement of Calvinism ever devised."[58] Vance reminds us that "Due to the close relationship between Church and state that existed at the time, the acceptance of Calvinism in England, culminating in the Westminster Assembly, is deeply intertwined with the civil and religious history of England."[59] A brief word about that history is therefore in order.

In the two preceding centuries, England had gone through a long struggle to escape Rome. At times she made progress, at other times she fell back into bondage. Henry VII had been proclaimed king in 1486 by a papal bull of Pope Innocent VIII. The Latin Vulgate was the official Bible. Wycliffe's Bible was suppressed, and the Provincial Council at Oxford in 1408 had forbidden the translation and printing of "any text of Holy Scripture into the English or other language...."[60] Henry VIII, who had written to Erasmus from London in 1511 that "many heretics furnish a daily holocaust,"[61] at the behest of Cromwell reversed himself and encouraged the Bible in English to be opened in every house and parish church—but a year before his death banned "the New Testament of Tyndale's or Coverdale's translation."[62]

During his brief reign, King Edward VI turned England away from Rome and welcomed Reformed theologians from the Continent into England, giving Calvinism a foothold there that it would never relinquish. In the late sixteenth century, the University of Cambridge became a Calvinist stronghold. Edward's sister, Mary I, daughter of Henry VIII, known as "Bloody Mary," succeeding him, brought England back under popery, forbade possession of any Protestant books, and burned at the stake hundreds who would not accept Rome's doctrines.

After Mary's death, the Geneva Bible came into use. Elizabeth I expelled the Jesuits from England. Under her, the Thirty-Nine Articles of the Church of England (mildly Calvinistic, but rejecting limited atonement) were formulated; they remain the official creed of that church to this day. John Knox held forth in Scotland, while the Puritans rose in England, only to be forced to conform by King James I, who gave us the King James Bible in 1611.

Charles I succeeded James. There were debates in Parliament over Calvinism, with its proponents gaining the upper hand. The Long Parliament ordered the printing of *A Display of Arminianism* by John Owen, which denounced Arminianism and upheld Limited Atonement. In the context of this tumultuous background and the continued partnership of the church with the state, the Westminster Assembly was convened by Parliament. The Parliament "waged a civil war against the king...abolished episcopacy, ejected two thousand royalist ministers...summoned the Westminster Assembly, executed Archbishop Laud, and eventually executed the king himself in 1649."[63]

Once again the deck was stacked. Westminster was not a gathering of those representing all true believers, but only of the Calvinists, who had gained the upper hand in Parliament. Today's boast is that "all of the Westminster divines were Calvinists."[64] Furthermore, as Vance wisely comments, "... like the Synod of Dort, the presence of government officials at an ostensibly religious assembly raises some questions about its legitimacy."[65] Expenses of the members were borne by the State. Even Calvinists admit, "The Assembly was the creature of Parliament and was never able to escape from Parliamentary supervision."[66]

Logan confesses, "The Assembly...was clearly and completely subservient to the political authority of Parliament."[67] De Witt also declares that the Assembly "was answerable, not to the King of Kings, but to the Lords and Commons of the English Parliament."[68] Schaff points out that "the Assembly... clung to the idea of a national state church, with a uniform system of doctrine, worship, and discipline, to which every man, woman, and child in three kingdoms should conform."[69] Bettany writes:

> In 1643 also the Westminster Assembly of divines
> was convened by Parliament to reform the Church of
> England "on the basis of the word of God, and to bring
> it into a nearer agreement with the Church of Scotland
> and the Reformed Churches on the Continent." The
> Scotch commissioners now required, as the price of

their co-operation with the English Parliament against Charles, the adoption of the Solemn League and Covenant [drawn by a Scottish revolutionary committee requiring signers to extirpate prelacy in all its forms in Scotland, Ireland and England]....

With this weapon...and the test of loyalty to the king, ejections of Episcopalians from their livings... amounted to some thousands.... So many vacancies were created that they could not be filled.... Finally the Westminster Assembly was ordered to draw up a scheme for ordination.... The Westminster Assembly laboured to evolve an acceptable scheme of Presbyterianism, the Independent members, however...proposing toleration for all sects....

The question soon arose...should presbyteries have the power of including or excluding members, or should each Independent congregation wield that power? Parliament undertook to settle the whole matter by ordaining that all persons aggrieved by the action of a presbytery might appeal to Parliament.... Cromwell in vain tried to reconcile Independents and Presbyterians. The latter predominated in Parliament, and in 1648 showed their continued intolerance by enacting that all who denied God, or the Trinity, or the atonement, or the canonical books of Scripture, or the resurrection of the dead and a final judgment were to 'suffer the pains of death, as in case of felony, without benefit of clergy.'... A long catalogue of heresies of the second class was specified, to be punished by imprisonment....[70]

Lessons to Be Learned

The so-called Reformation synods and councils and the confessions and decrees they generated, which many Calvinists today honor as stating the true doctrine of Christ, were promoted by an established state church in partnership with the civil rulers—contrary to the Word of God. Always the overriding concern was for unity, and those who did not agree with the majority position were silenced, persecuted, imprisoned, banished, and sometimes executed.

Just as the Roman Catholic Church had persecuted and killed those who did not agree with her down through the centuries, so the newly established Protestant churches began to do the same. Anabaptists, for example, were persecuted and killed by both Catholics and Protestants because the latter still believed in Augustine's baptism of infants into the family of God, with its magical powers of regeneration—a Roman Catholic heresy that clung to Luther and Calvin and that clings to most of their followers to this day.

History clearly records that these were the men and the motives behind the established creeds and confessions. Unquestionably, their *modus operandi* followed in the footsteps of Constantine. Not a true Christian, and thus not interested in truth but in the "unity" of the empire, Constantine used "Christianity" to that end. Under him, the church, once persecuted by the world, became the persecutor. True Christians were still the ones being persecuted. The only change was that an oppressive church had joined the world to persecute those not subscribing to its dogmas.

The new persecution was done in the name of Christ but was the very antithesis of all Christ taught and lived, and for which He died. Following in the footsteps of Rome, which in most matters they opposed, the Protestant churches continued the same practice. We cannot, and dare not, ignore these facts in evaluating "Reformation" creeds and statements of faith that came from councils and synods called by the state for the sake of unity.

Augustine had been happy to use the state in an unbiblical partnership to enforce "faith" upon heretics. Driven by the same belief, Calvin used the same system in Geneva. Nor can one deny the obvious relationship between this forcing of "faith" upon the unwilling, and the two major doctrines of both Augustine and Calvin—Total Depravity and double Predestination with their concomitant denial of any genuine choice for mankind with regard to God and salvation. Freedom of conscience was the natural victim, a form of oppression that even the unsaved can tolerate only for so long.

Defining Calvinism

In spite of many differences of opinion among Calvinists today, Calvinism is generally explained by the acronym, TULIP. Philip F. Congdon writes that "a tulip is a beautiful flower, but bad theology. The fruit of the flower is appealing; the fruit of the theology is appalling...works, as an *inevitable result*, are necessary for salvation. To be fair, Classical Calvinists usually object to this by describing the gospel message as *not* 'faith + works = justification,' but 'faith = justification + works'.... This is no more than a word game. It is best seen in the old Calvinist saying: 'You are saved by faith alone, but the faith that saves you is never alone....'"[71]

Some readers may have never heard of **TULIP**. Others, though knowing that it has something to do with Calvinism, find it difficult to remember what each letter stands for. Here, in brief, is a summary of common explanations. In each case, in order to avoid the charge that they are not properly stated, they are presented in the words of the major Calvinistic creeds or confessions:

> **"T" stands for Total Depravity:** that man, because he is spiritually dead to God "in trespasses and in sins" (Ephesians 2:1; Colossians 2:13), is incapable of responding to the gospel, though able to make other moral choices.
>
> The Westminster Confession of Faith declares, "Our first parents...became dead in sin, and wholly defiled in all the faculties and parts of soul and body... wholly inclined to all evil.... Man, by his fall into a state of sin, hath wholly lost all ability of will to any spiritual good accompanying salvation...being altogether averse from that good, and dead to sin, is not able by his own strength, to convert himself, or to prepare himself thereunto."[72]
>
> **"U" stands for Unconditional Election:** that God decides on no basis whatsoever but by the mystery of His will to save some, called the elect, and to allow all others to go to hell, even though He *could* save *all* mankind if He so desired.
>
> The Canons of Dort declare, "That some receive the gift of faith from God, and others do not receive it proceeds from God's eternal decree...[by] which decree,

he graciously softens the hearts of the elect, however obstinate, and inclines them to believe, while he leaves the non-elect in his just judgment to their own wickedness and obduracy."[73]

"L" stands for Limited Atonement: that the elect are the only ones for whom Christ died in payment of the penalty for their sins, and that His death is efficacious for no others, nor was intended to be.

Dort declares: "For this was the sovereign counsel, and most gracious will and purpose of God the Father, that...the most precious death of his Son should extend to all the elect...all those, and those only, who were from eternity chosen to salvation...he purchased by his death."[74]

"I" stands for Irresistible Grace: that God is able to cause whomever He will to respond to the gospel; that without this enabling, no one could do so; and that He only provides this Irresistible Grace to the elect and damns the rest.

The Westminster Confession states: "All those whom God hath predestinated unto life, and those only, he is pleased, in his appointed and accepted time, effectually to call, by his Word and Spirit, out of that state of sin and death...effectually drawing them to Jesus Christ; yet so, as they come most freely, being made willing by his grace."[75]

"P" stands for Perseverance of the Saints: that God will not allow any of the elect to fail to persevere in living a life consistent with the salvation that He has sovereignly given them.

The Westminster Confession states: "They, whom God hath accepted in his Beloved, effectually called, and sanctified by His Spirit, can neither totally nor finally fall away from the state of grace, but shall certainly persevere therein to the end, and be eternally saved. This perseverance of the saints depends not upon their own free will, but upon the immutability of the decree of election."[76]

William Cunningham speaks for most Calvinists when he writes that "No synod or council was ever held in the church, whose decisions, all things considered, are entitled to more deference and respect [than the Synod of Dort]."[77]

With all due respect, I would suggest that the Bible alone is our authority, not the beliefs of either John Calvin or Jacobus Arminius, or any council, synod, assembly, or creed. In the following pages, the points of TULIP are compared with the Bible, one point at a time, and in order.

1. George Park Fisher, *History of the Christian Church*, (New York: Charles Scribner's Sons, 1902), 406.

2. Jacobus Arminius, *The Works of James Arminius,* trans. James and William Nichols (Grand Rapids, MI: Baker Book House, 1986), 1:26.

3. From the old *Edinburgh Encyclopedia* (Scotland: n. p., n. d.); quoted in Arminius, *Works,* 1:306.

4. Laurence M. Vance, *The Other Side of Calvinism* (Pensacola, FL: Vance Publications, rev. ed., 1999), 126.

5. Arminius, *Works,* 2:243–44.

6. Ibid., 2:264–65.

7. Ibid., 1:298.

8. Ibid., 299.

9. Ibid.,644.

10. Ibid., 2:115–18, 138, 141–43, 145, etc.

11. Ibid.,379.

12. Ibid., 141.

13. Ibid., 443.

14. Ibid., 387–88.

15. Ibid., 157, 256; 1:659–60.

16. Ibid., 1:102.

17. *The Works of James Arminius, Vols. 1 & 2*, Translated from the Latin by James Nichols: "The Apology or Defense of James Arminius, against certain theological articles extensively distributed and currently circulated... in the low countries and beyond... in which both Arminius, and Adrian Borrius, a minister of Leyden, are rendered suspected of novelty and heterodoxy, of error and heresy, on the subject of religion," probably published early in 1609 shortly before his death. See also, *A Declaration of the Sentiments of Arminius—on Predestination, Divine Providence, the freedom of the will, the grace of God, the Divinity of the Son of God, and the justification of man before God.* Delivered before the states of Holland, at the Hague, on the thirtieth of October, 1608.

18. R. K. McGregor Wright, *No Place for Sovereignty: What's Wrong with Freewill Theism* (Downer's Grove, IL: InterVarsity Press, 1996), 29.

19. Joseph C. Dillow, *The Reign of the Servant Kings: A Study of Eternal Security and the Final Significance of Man* (Haysville, NC: Schoettle Publishing Co., 2nd ed. 1993), 266.

20. J. I. Packer, "*Sola Fide*: The Reformed Doctrine of Justification" (http://www.the-highway.com/Justification_Packer.html).

21. Henry C. Sheldon, *History of Christian Doctrine* (New York: Harper and Bros., 2nd ed. 1895), 2:34–35.

22. George L. Curtiss, *Arminianism in History* (New York: Cranston and Curts, 1894), 10.

23. Arminius, *Works*, 1:103.

24. Ibid., 2:81.

25. Ibid., 623.

26. E. H. Broadbent, *The Pilgrim Church* (Port Colborne, ON: Gospel Folio Press, reprint 1999), 255.

27. Samuel Fisk, *Calvinistic Paths Retraced* (Raleigh, NC: Biblical Evangelism Press, 1985), 120.

28. John T. McNeil, *Makers of the Christian Tradition* (San Francisco: Harper and Row, 1964), 221.

29. Arminius, *Works*, 1:329; 2:472–73.

30. Ibid., 1:248.

31. Ibid., 316–17.

32. Ibid., 1:254; 2:497.

33. Earle E. Cairns, *Christianity Through the Centuries: A History of the Christian Church,* revised and enlarged ed. (Grand Rapids, MI: Zondervan, 1981), 325.

34. Albert H. Newman, *A Manual of Church History* (Philadelphia, PA: American Baptist Publication Society, 1933), 2:340.

35. John Owen, *A Display of Arminianism*, "To the right honourable, The Lords and Gentlemen of the Committee for Religion," and "To the Christian Reader" in *The Works of John Owen*, ed. William Goold (The Banner of Truth Trust, 1978) X: 7-8.

36. Ibid., 4.

37. McGregor, *No Place*, 28.

38. Eusebius Pamphilius of Caesaria, advisor to Constantine, *The Life of Constantine* (n. p., c. A.D. 335), 3.62.

39. Philip Schaff, *History of the Christian Church* (New York: Charles Scribner, 1910; Grand Rapids, MI: Wm B. Eerdmans Publishing Co., reprint 1959), 142.

40. Ibid.

41. William Jones, *The History of the Christian Church* (Church History Research and Archives, 5th ed. 1983), 1:306.

42. David Gay, *Battle for the Church: 1517–1644* (Lowestoft, UK: Brachus, 1997), 44.

43. Zane C. Hodges, "The New Puritanism, Pt. 2: Michael S. Horton: Holy War with Unholy Weapons," *Journal of the Grace Evangelical Society*, Spring 1994, 6:11.

44. Curtiss, *Arminianism.*, 69.

45. Vance, *Other Side*, 151–52.

46. From "The Opinions of the Remonstrants" (presented at Dordrecht, Holland), 1619.

47. A. W. Tozer, "The Sovereignty of God" (Camp Hill, PA: Christian Publications, 1997), Audiotape.

48. Quoted in full in Vance, *Other Side*, 153–54.

49. Quoted in Arminius, *Works*, I: lxiii.

50. Vance, *Other Side*, 158–59.

51. Herman Hanko, "Total Depravity," in Herman Hanko, Homer C. Hoeksema, and Gise J. Van Baren, *The Five Points of Calvinism* (Grandville, MI: Reformed Free Publishing Association, 1976), 10.

52. Arthur C. Custance, *The Sovereignty of Grace* (Phillipsburg, NJ: Presbyterian and Reformed Publishing Co., 1979), 71.

53. Cairns, *Christianity,* 325.

54. Cited in Vance, *Other Side*, 148.

55. Louis Berkhof, *The History of Christian Doctrines* (Grand Rapids, MI: Baker Book House, 1937), 152.

56. Homer Hoeksema, *The Voice of Our Fathers* (Grandville, MI: Reformed Free Publishing Association, 1980), 114.

57. William Cunningham, *The Reformers and the Theology of the Reformation* (Carlisle, PA: Banner of Truth Trust, 1967), 2:381; cited in Vance, *Other Side*, 153.

58. M. Howard Rienstra, "The History and Development of Calvinism in Scotland and England," in Bratt, ed., *The Rise and Development of Calvinism*, 110; cited in Vance, *Other Side*, 159.

59. Vance, *Other Side*.

60. Alfred W. Pollard, ed., *Records of the English Bible* (Oxford: Oxford University Press, 1911), 1.

61. H. Maynard Smith, *Pre-Reformation England* (New York: Russell and Russell, 1963), 289.

62. Paul L. Hughes and James F. Larkin, eds., *Tudor Royal Proclamations* (New Haven, CT: Yale University Press, 1964), 1:374.

63. Vance, *Other Side*, 167.

64. William S. Barker, "The Men and Parties of the Assembly," in John L. Carson and David W. Hall, eds., *To Glorify and Enjoy God: A Commemoration of the 350th Anniversary of the Westminster Assembly*, 52; cited in Vance, *Other Side*, 171.

65. Vance, *Other Side*, 172.

66. John T. McNeil, *The History and Character of Calvinism* (Oxford: Oxford University Press, 1966), 324.

67. Samuel T. Logan, "The Context and Work of the Assembly," in Carson and Hall, *To Glorify*, 36.

68. John R. de Witt, "The Form of Church Government," in Carson and Hall, *To Glorify*, 148.

69. Philip Schaff, *The Creeds of Christendom* (Grand Rapids, MI: Baker Book House, 1990), 1:730.

70. G. T. Bettany, *A Popular History of the Reformation and Modern Protestantism* (London: Ward, Lock and Bowden, Ltd, 1895), 414–20.

71. Philip F. Congdon, "Soteriological Implications of Five-point Calvinism," *Journal of the Grace Evangelical Society*, Autumn 1995, 8:15, 55–68.

72. Westminster Confession of Faith (London: n. p., 1643), VI: i, ii, iv; IX: iii.

73. Canons of Dort (Dordrecht, Holland, 1619), 1:6.

74. Ibid., II:8.

75. Westminster, X:I.

76. Ibid., XVII: i, ii.

77. William Cunningham, *Historical Theology* (Edmonton, AB: Still Waters Revival Books, n. d.), 2:379.

"T" is for "Total Depravity"

OF THE TEN WORDS making up the acronym TULIP, four (total, depravity, unconditional, and irresistible) are not even found in the Bible, and two (limited and perseverance) are each found only once. As for the phrases expressed by each letter (Total Depravity, Unconditional Election, Limited Atonement, Irresistible Grace, and Perseverance of the Saints), *none* of them appears anywhere from the beginning of Genesis to the end of Revelation.

We have, therefore, good cause to be at least cautious in approaching these key Calvinist concepts. The burden is upon their promoters to show that these ideas, in spite of their absence from Scripture, are indeed taught there. "Trinity" likewise does not occur, but it is clearly taught.

Calvinism offers a special definition of human depravity: that depravity equals inability—and this special definition necessitates both Unconditional Election and Irresistible Grace. As the Canons of Dort declare, "Therefore all men...without the regenerating grace of the Holy Spirit...are neither able nor willing to return to God...nor to dispose themselves to reformation."[1] That declaration expresses human opinion—it is never stated in the Bible.

Calvinism insists that all men, being totally depraved by nature, are *unable* to repent and believe the gospel, yet holds us accountable for failing to do so. How can it reasonably be said that a person is unwilling to do what he is unable to do? There is no way either to prove or to disprove the statement.

Can we say that a man is *unwilling* to fly like a bird? If he were able, he might very well be willing. Certainly his alleged unwillingness to fly like a bird cannot be blamed as the reason he doesn't do so! Nor can he be held accountable for failing to fly so long as flying is impossible for him. Isn't Calvinism guilty of both absurdity and injustice by declaring man to be incapable of repentance and faith, then condemning him for failing to repent and believe?

Calvinism's Undeniable Irrationality

Such glaring contradictions are innate within Calvinism and have caused divisions even among Calvinists, who cannot all agree among themselves. Consider the controversy in 1945 over the fitness for ordination of Gordon H. Clark. "Cornelius Van Til led the seminary faculty in a *Complaint* against Clark's understanding of the Confession of Faith."[2] Clark was accused of "rationalism" for his unwillingness to declare (as so-called "moderate" Calvinists do) that salvation was sincerely offered by God to those for whom Christ, according to Calvinism, did not die and whom God had from eternity past predestined to eternal torment. Clark considered it to be a direct contradiction that God could seek the salvation of those "He has from eternity determined not to save."

Clark was accused by so-called moderates of being a "hyper-Calvinist"—but such labels are misleading. Both Clark and his "moderate" opponents believed exactly the same—that God had predestined some to heaven and others to hell. Clark was simply being honest in admitting that it could not rationally be said that God "loves" those He could save but doesn't. "Moderate" Calvinism is thus guilty of an undeniable contradiction, yet John MacArthur spends an entire book trying to support this contradiction.[3] As we shall see, the "moderates" hide their irrationality behind the idea that God is "free" to love different people with different kinds of love—forgetting that any kind of genuine love is loving, and that it is not loving to damn those who could be saved.

A similar controversy, which originated among the faculty at Calvin Seminary, "had plagued the Christian Reformed Church during the 1920s...[and in 1924] ended with the exodus of the Calvinists from the Christian Reformed Church under the leadership of Herman Hoeksema, and the formation of a new church, the Protestant Reformed Church."[4] Van Til, in disagreement with the Westminster Confession, argued that Clark was making "logic rule over Scripture...." Van Til insisted that Scripture contains irreconcilable paradoxes that "have of necessity the appearance of being contradictory."[5]

If that is the case, then Scripture is irrational and cannot be defended reasonably; yet God offers to reason with man (Isaiah

1:18). Peter tells us that we must always be ready to give an answer to everyone who asks a *reason* for our faith (1 Peter 3:15) and Paul "reasoned" with the Jews (Acts 18:4,19).

Attempting to escape the irrationality of blaming the non-elect for failing to do what they can't do, some Calvinists insist that man is able but simply not willing to turn to Christ. This is a minority view that contradicts Total Depravity and it is partially correct. The problem with sinners is indeed unwillingness. For a person to be unwilling, however, he must have a will, and thus by an act of that will could become willing—a fact that Calvinism denies. Furthermore, Calvin and his followers have declared in the clearest language that man is unable to believe the gospel, to turn to Christ, or to seek God or good: "He is free to turn to Christ, but not able."[6] Inability is certainly the major view.

There is not a verse in the Bible, however, that presents Calvinism's radical idea that the sinner is incapable of believing the very gospel that offers him forgiveness and salvation, and yet he is condemned by God for failing to believe. In fact, as we shall see, the Bible declares otherwise. "All men everywhere" (Acts 17:30) are repeatedly called upon to repent and to believe on Christ. One would never derive from Scripture the idea that the unregenerate are unable to believe. Dave Breese, highly respected and brilliant author and expositor of Scripture, declared that it "cannot be shown that 'total depravity' is in fact a scriptural truth."[7]

Yet Talbot and Crampton write, "The Bible stresses the total inability of fallen man to respond to the things of God.... This is what the Calvinist refers to as 'total depravity.'"[8] Palmer calls this doctrine "the most central issue between the Arminian and the Calvinist, what Martin Luther even said was the hinge on which the whole Reformation turned."[9]

Consequently, the Calvinist insists that regeneration must precede faith—and thus it must precede salvation, which is by faith alone: "once he [the sinner] is born again, he can for the first time turn to Jesus...asking Jesus to save him."[10] What strange and unbiblical doctrine is this, that a sinner must be born again before he can believe the gospel! Is it not through believing the gospel that we are born again (1 Peter 1:23-25)? R. C. Sproul declares, "A cardinal point of Reformed theology is the maxim, 'Regeneration precedes faith.'"[11]

Nowhere in Scripture, however, is there a suggestion that man must be *regenerated before* he can be saved by faith in Christ. Indeed, many scriptures declare the opposite, for example: "...to make thee wise unto salvation through faith which is in Christ Jesus" (2 Timothy 3:15), and "ye are all the children of God by faith in Christ Jesus" (Galatians 3:26). Faith *always* precedes salvation/regeneration. There is not one scripture that states clearly the doctrine that regeneration comes first and then faith follows—*not one*. We will deal with this key doctrine in more depth later.

Spurgeon, though a Calvinist, said, "A man who is regenerated is saved."[12] John MacArthur also equates being saved and regenerated.[13] Calvin correctly declared, "Every man from the commencement of his faith, becomes a Christian...."[14] But if the elect must be regenerated before they have faith, their regeneration still leaves them non-Christians, since a man is saved by faith and thereby becomes a Christian (John 6:47; 11:25; 20:31; Acts 16:31; Romans 1:16; 10:9; 1 Corinthians 1:21; Hebrews 10:39; etc.). What "regeneration" is this that doesn't save? Spurgeon did not accept this part of Calvinism and therefore said it was "ridiculous" to preach Christ to the regenerate.[15] Of course. Contradicting the teaching of "regeneration precedes faith" so popular among Calvinists today, Calvin even titled a chapter, "Regeneration by Faith."[16]

Nevertheless, viewing depravity as inability, which necessitates regeneration before salvation, is the very foundation of most of today's Calvinism. Engelsma acknowledges, "Deny this doctrine and the whole of Calvinism is demolished."[17] To be fair, we must, says Engelsma, "let Calvinism speak for itself."[18] That is why we so extensively quote so many Calvinists.

Inasmuch as Total Depravity requires regeneration *before* faith or salvation, many Calvinists assume it could take place—and probably does—in infancy. Thus Hoeksema reasons that "regeneration can take place in the smallest of infants…in the sphere of the covenant of God, He usually regenerates His elect children from infancy."[19] Do the children of Calvinists then behave in a sanctified way far different from other children? Hardly.

There we have one more declaration that regeneration leaves a person still unsaved, insomuch as salvation is by faith, and infants neither can understand nor believe the gospel, which is a clear requirement for salvation. We ask Calvinists, in all sincerity, where this strange doctrine is stated in the Bible. None of them has ever answered that question.

Depravity Equals Inability?

Most Christians, if asked whether man is by nature totally depraved, would likely respond in the affirmative. However, the Calvinists' view of the obvious sinfulness of mankind goes far beyond the average Christian's ordinary understanding of depravity. As another leading Calvinist states, "Paul's assessment of persons apart from Christ may justly be summed up in the theological categories of 'total depravity' and 'total inability.'"[20]

"Inability"? A person may be unable to walk, or to think properly, or to enter a restricted area. In each case the person is prevented in some way from doing what he otherwise could do. Calvinism, however, does not admit to a normal ability that some are prevented from using. It asserts a universal and unique incapacity: that *no one* can believe the gospel without being sovereignly regenerated by God. Nowhere in the Bible, however, is this proposition clearly stated. Yet this is Calvinism's very foundation, from which the other four points flow.

The Bible repeatedly presents man's sinfulness and warns that rejecting the salvation God has provided in Christ leaves the sinner to suffer eternal punishment under the wrath of God. Never, however, does the Bible suggest that because of Adam's original sin all of his descendants lack the capacity to turn to God through faith in Christ. Much less does Scripture teach that God only gives the "ability" to believe the gospel to a certain select group. Instead, the Bible is filled with invitations to all men to repent and believe on Christ to the saving of their souls—and warnings that if they refuse to do so they will suffer God's wrath eternally. Paul went everywhere, preaching to everyone he encountered throughout the Roman Empire "repentance toward God, and faith toward our Lord Jesus Christ" (Acts 20:21). Apparently, he believed that anyone could respond—not just a certain elect whom God had sovereignly regenerated and then given them faith to believe.

Clearly, *all* are *commanded* to repent and turn to Christ. As Paul declared on Mars' Hill in Athens, God "commandeth all men everywhere to repent" (Acts 17:30). To say that God commands men to do what they cannot do without His grace, then withholds the grace they need and punishes them eternally for failing to obey, is to make a mockery of God's Word, of His mercy and love, and is to libel His character. Not inability but unwillingness is man's problem: "The wicked, through the pride of his countenance, will not seek after God" (Psalm 10:4). Christ rebuked the rabbis, "And ye *will not* come to me, that ye might have life" (John 5:40) —an unjust accusation to level at those who *could not* come unless God caused them to do so.

It is neither stated in Scripture, nor does it follow reasonably, that anyone, as a result of his depravity, even if his every thought is evil, is thereby unable to believe the glad tidings of the gospel and receive Christ as his Savior. Here, once again, we find Augustine's influence. As noted earlier, it is claimed that Augustine was "perhaps the first after Paul to realize the Total Depravity of man;"[21] indeed, that Augustine invented "the exaggerated doctrine of total human depravity...."[22] One often wonders whether Calvin relied more upon Augustine than upon the Bible.

Turning depravity into inability leads inevitably to points 2 and 4: that God must unconditionally elect those who will be saved; and that He must effect that work through Irresistible Grace. Yet even the claim of inability turns out to be misleading.

What Ability Is Needed to Receive a Gift?

The Bible makes it clear that salvation is the *gift* of God through Jesus Christ, and that it is offered to all mankind: "... by the righteousness of one [Christ] the *free gift* came upon *all men* unto justification of life" (Romans 5:18; emphases added). No one can purchase, earn, or merit salvation. It must be (and need only be) received as a *free* gift. What ability is required to accept a gift? Only the capacity to choose—something that daily experience proves is normal to every human being, even to the smallest child. How, then, is it possible for any sinner to lack the "ability" to be saved?

Of course, the natural mind is at enmity with God. We are rebellious sinners bent upon taking our own way and blinded by the deceitfulness of our own lusts. But not one of the many scriptures that describe man's depravity state that he is impervious to the convicting power of the Holy Spirit—or *no one* could be saved. Nor does any scripture declare that God convicts and convinces only an elect group. Rather, the Spirit of truth convinces "the world of sin, and of righteousness, and of judgment..." (John 16:8).

Unquestionably, to receive the gift of salvation one must simply believe the gospel. Moreover, the very command, "Go ye into all the world, and preach the gospel to every creature" (Mark 16:15) implies the ability of *every* person to believe the gospel. Indeed, that everyone knows the truth of God's existence, his moral responsibility to God, and his breach of the moral laws, is stated repeatedly in Scripture:

- The heavens declare the glory of God; and the firmament sheweth his handywork.... There is no speech nor language, where their voice is not heard. (Psalm 19:1–3)

- If any man thirst, let him come unto me, and drink. (John 7:37)

- Whosoever will, let him take the water of life freely. (Revelation 22:17)

- For the wrath of God is revealed from heaven against all ungodliness and unrighteousness of men, who hold the truth in unrighteousness; because that which may be known of God is manifest in them; for God hath shewed it unto them. For the invisible things of him from the creation of the world are clearly seen, being understood by the things that are made, even his eternal power and Godhead; so that they are without excuse.... (Romans 1:18–22)

- For when the Gentiles, which have not the law, do by nature the things contained in the law, these, having not the law [i.e., given to the Jews through Moses],... shew the work of the law written in their hearts, their conscience also bearing witness, and their thoughts the mean while accusing or else excusing one another.... (Romans 2:14–15)

- Believe on the Lord Jesus Christ, and thou shalt be saved... (Acts 16:31)

In 1 Corinthians 2:7–16, Paul refers to "the things of the Spirit of God [which] are spiritually discerned...the hidden wisdom [concerning] the things which God hath prepared for them that love him...the deep things of God...which the Holy Ghost

teacheth [which] are spiritually discerned." The Calvinist uses
this passage to support his idea of "total depravity"—i.e., that
only the elect who have been regenerated can understand and
believe the gospel. Paul, however, is here speaking of more than
the simple gospel; he is referring to the deeper understanding of
spiritual truth that comes with maturity in Christ. That fact, if
not understood from what we have just quoted, is crystal clear
from his next words: "And I, brethren, could not speak unto
you as unto spiritual, but as unto carnal, even as unto babes in
Christ. I have fed you with milk, and not with meat: for hitherto
ye were not able to bear it…" (1 Corinthians 3:1–2).

Nevertheless, even if he were speaking only of the gospel,
this passage could not be used to support the teaching of total
inability of the natural man to believe. Of course, no one can
understand the gospel except by the enlightening of the Holy
Spirit. But neither here nor elsewhere does Paul even hint (much
less state plainly) that the Holy Spirit only reveals the gospel to
an elect group. He declares that the "gospel is hid to them that
are lost" because "the god of this world [Satan] hath blinded the
minds of them which believe not…" (2 Corinthians 4:3,4)—an
effort Satan would not need to expend if all men were totally
depraved and thus totally unable to believe the gospel.

Furthermore, Paul clearly states that "the grace of God
that bringeth salvation hath appeared to all men" (Titus 2:11).
Similarly, Christ (as just noted), declared that the Holy Spirit,
"the Spirit of truth," would "reprove the world of sin, and
of righteousness, and of judgment" (John 16:8). The New
King James translates "reprove" as "convict." John MacArthur
explains this as "conviction of the need for the Savior."[23]
It is clear from the context that Christ means the entire world

of sinners, not that the conviction of the need of a Savior is only for an elect whom He has predestined for eternity in heaven.

Just as no special ability is required on the part of the endangered person to be rescued from drowning or from a burning building, or on the part of the imprisoned criminal who is pardoned to accept his release, so no unusual ability is required of the person whom Christ rescues from eternal condemnation. Thus, Calvinism's very foundation in its special definition of human depravity as inability is as unreasonable as it is unbiblical.

Born Again Before Salvation?

Explaining Calvinism carefully, Palmer reiterates that no man can under-stand the gospel and that this "lack of understanding is also a part of man's depravity...all minds are blind, unless they are regenerated."[24] The thoroughly Calvinistic London Baptist Confession of 1689 stated, "As a consequence of his fall into a state of sin, man...is not able, by any strength of his own, to turn himself to God, or even to prepare himself to turn to God."[25] On the contrary, man's problem is *not* inability but unwillingness: "ye will not hear...will not believe...(Habakkuk 1:5; Acts 3:23). There are too many scriptures to list, but here are several more: Isaiah 7:9; Zechariah 14:17; Malachi 2:2; Matthew 18:16; Luke 9:5, 19:14, 22:67; John 4:48; Acts 22:18; 2 Timothy 4:3, and others.

James White devotes an entire chapter to "The Inabilities of Man." He recites a long list of man's sins, of his evil, of his depravity, and explains that he is a "*fallen creature*, a slave to sin, spiritually dead, incapable of doing what is pleasing to God."

He cites many scriptures concerning man's estrangement from God and the deceitfulness of his heart, that he can no more change his heart than the leopard can change his spots, that his mind is hostile toward God, that no man can come to Christ except the Father draw him, and so forth. White declares, "The Reformed assertion is that man cannot understand *and embrace* the gospel nor respond in *faith and repentance* toward Christ without God first freeing him from sin and giving him spiritual life (regeneration)."[26] Nowhere, however, does he cite a scripture that declares the most wretched sinner's *inability* to believe the gospel or to receive the free gift of eternal life that God offers to all.

There are, of course, many scriptures describing man's evil heart and practices. None, however, states that a man cannot believe the gospel unless he is one of the elect and has been given that faith by a sovereign act of God. Pink declares that "the sinner, of himself, *cannot* repent and believe."[27]

Here the Calvinist comes dangerously close to teaching salvation by works. If there is no *work* I must do to be saved, then how can I lack the *ability* to do it? And surely no one lacks the ability simply to believe!

For all of their insistence upon man's inability to believe the gospel and to receive Christ, however, Calvinists cannot agree among themselves. J. I. Packer contradicts his fellow Calvinists (and what he himself says elsewhere) in declaring that adoption (i.e., regeneration) *follows* faith and justification: "God elected men from eternity in order that in due time they might be justified, upon their believing. Their adoption as God's sons follows upon their justification; it is, indeed, no more than the positive outworking of God's justifying sentence."[28]

Of course, Packer, like other Calvinists, would deny that he is contradicting himself. How? He would argue that "regeneration" (as Calvinism defines it) is not the same as justification, or being adopted as sons and daughters into God's family. But if "regeneration" is not being "born again" as Christ described it to Nicodemus, but leaves the sinner, though regenerated, still unjustified before God, we demand to know where in Scripture this Calvinist "regeneration" is presented. In fact, it is not biblical at all.

As we have seen, defining depravity as inability requires God to sovereignly *regenerate* man, and without any recognition, understanding, or faith on man's part, raise him from being "dead in trespasses and sins" (Ephesians 2:1) to spiritual life. Only then can He give man the faith to believe the gospel. As Dort, quoted above, says, "Without the regenerating grace of the Holy Spirit, they are neither able nor willing to return to God...."[29] *Enabling* grace is needed for faith, but not *"regenerating* grace." Where does the Bible say one must be *regenerated* before one can believe the gospel? Not one verse can be cited in which that proposition is stated clearly.

Most non-Calvinists have thought that being "born again," as Christ presented it to Nicodemus in John 3, is the same as being saved. Therefore, they are surprised to learn that Calvinism teaches that one must experience the new birth, which Christ describes in John 3, *before* one can believe the gospel and be saved. As Sproul emphasizes once again, "The Reformed view of predestination teaches that before a person can choose Christ...he must be born again...one does not first believe, then become reborn...."[30]

On the contrary, we are "born again" by believing "the word

which by the gospel is preached…" (1 Peter: 1:23–25). In fact, the Bible always presents faith as the condition of salvation.

The Disturbing Consequences

Sadly, the acceptance of this theory leads to a corollary that is even more unbiblical as well as contradictory to the innate sense of compassion that God has placed within even unregenerate man: that God *could* save all mankind but deliberately withholds from multitudes the salvation He gives to the elect. Obviously, what God does for the elect (who likewise were "totally depraved" by nature) He could do for all, if He so desired. That He doesn't would prove that the One who *is love* lacks love for all mankind—which is contrary to *all* Scripture: "Who will have all men to be saved, and to come unto the knowledge of the truth" (1 Timothy 2:4).

If lost sinners suffer from such an inability that they can be saved only by God's sovereign act of regeneration (and all men are not saved), it follows that God limits His mercy and grace to a *select group*. As one of the most fervent Calvinists, Arthur W. Pink, writes to the elect, "Then do you not see that it is due to no lack of power in God…that *other rebels* are not saved too? If God was able to subdue *your* will and win *your* heart, and that *without* interfering with your moral responsibility, then is He not able to do the same for others [i.e., the non-elect]? Assuredly He is." [31]

Here we confront a major problem with Calvinism: its denial of God's infinite love for all. That God, who repeatedly declares His love for all mankind, would choose to save only some and leave all others to suffer eternal damnation would be contrary to His very nature of infinite love and mercy as the

Bible presents Him. Yet the very damnation of perhaps billions is said by the Calvinist to have been foreordained from eternity past because it pleases and glorifies God! The Westminster Confession of Faith, paraphrasing Calvin himself, declares that God ordains to eternal punishment multitudes whom He *could* just as well ordain to eternal life and joy in heaven:

> By the decree of God, for the manifestation of his glory, some men and angels are predestinated unto everlasting life; and others foreordained to everlasting death.... Those of mankind that are predestinated unto life, God...hath chosen in Christ unto everlasting glory...to the praise of his glorious grace.... The rest of mankind, God was pleased, according to the unsearchable counsel of his own will...for the glory of his sovereign power over his creatures...to ordain them to dishonor and wrath for their sin, to the praise of his glorious justice.[32]

Even Sproul admits, "If some people are not elected unto salvation then it would seem that God is not at all that loving toward them. Further, it seems that it would have been more loving of God not to have allowed them to be born. That may indeed be the case."[33] God's love, however, is infinite and perfect. It is therefore an oxymoron to suggest that God was ever toward anyone "not all that loving" and might "have been more loving." No Calvinist has ever satisfactorily explained the lack of love with which they charge God. Who could fail to be gravely concerned for this gross misrepresentation of our loving Creator?!

The great Apostle Paul could declare unequivocally, "I am not ashamed of the gospel of Christ!" It almost sounds as though

Sproul has some reservations concerning the gospel according to Calvinism. If the gospel is not good news to everyone, but only to the elect, is that cause for us to be ashamed of a God who is less than loving to all? Paul did not have the problem of believing that God was "not all that loving."

By now it should be clear that Calvinism is founded upon the premise that God does not love everyone, is not merciful to all, does not want all to be saved, but in fact is pleased to damn billions whom, by sovereign regeneration, He could have saved had He so desired. If that is the God of the Bible, Calvinism is true. If that is not the God of the Bible, who "is love" (1 John 4:8), Calvinism is false. The central issue is God's love and character in relation to mankind, as presented in Scripture. The very title of this book, *What Love Is This?*, asks of Calvinism a question to which it has no answer.

As we have already pointed out, Spurgeon (whom Calvinists love to quote when he supports Calvinism) found himself in deep conflict. He urged everyone to come to Christ—yet to do so contradicted his affirmation of Limited Atonement. In effect, Spurgeon was urging men to come to Christ, even though he didn't believe Christ had died for them. Yet conscience and knowledge of God would not allow him to escape the fact that, just as God commands all mankind to "love your neighbor as yourself," so God must genuinely love all mankind.

As we have previously noted, in reference to 1 Timothy 2:4, Spurgeon declared: "As it is *my* wish…[and] *your* wish…so it is God's wish that all men should be saved….. He is no less benevolent than we are."[34] Spurgeon was caught in the web of contradictions woven by Calvinism. How could God, whose sovereignty enables Him to do anything He desires (a corner-stone of Calvinism), fail to save those He "wishes" to be saved?

Which Comes First—Salvation or Faith?

Nowhere, from Genesis to Revelation, does the Bible teach that sinful man, without first being regenerated, is incapable of repenting of his sins, turning to God, and believing the gospel to the saving of his soul. On the contrary, it is all too clear that faith precedes salvation and is in fact a *condition* of salvation. There are scores of verses declaring that we are saved through faith, through believing on the Lord Jesus Christ as He is presented in the gospel. This sequence of events is undeniable:

- He that believeth...shall be saved.... (Mark 16:16)

- Then cometh the devil, and taketh away the word out of their hearts, lest they should believe and be saved.... (Luke 8:12)

- Believe on the Lord Jesus Christ, and thou shalt be saved.... (Acts 16:31)

- I am not ashamed of the gospel of Christ: for it is the power of God unto salvation to every one that believeth.... (Romans 1:16)

- Moreover, brethren, I declare unto you the gospel...by which also ye are saved...unless ye have believed in vain. (1 Corinthians 15:1–2)

- For by grace are ye saved through faith.... (Ephesians 2:8)

- ...them which should hereafter believe on him to life ever-lasting. (1 Timothy 1:16)

These scriptures are clear. Therefore, in order to support "regeneration before faith," it must be proved that regeneration leaves one still unsaved and thus under God's judgment. But that view is both unbiblical and irrational.

In numerous places, the Bible declares that upon believing in Christ according to the gospel (and *only* by believing), we receive eternal life from God as a free gift: "That whosoever believeth in him should...have everlasting life (John 3:16); He that heareth...and believeth...hath everlasting life... (5:24); That ye might believe that Jesus is the Christ, the Son of God; and that believing ye might have life through his name" (20:31). Believing is obviously a condition for receiving the gift of eternal life. Could one be "regenerated" and remain unsaved and without "life through his name," which is received by faith alone? Not according to the Bible! How, then, could regeneration precede faith?

The Bible clearly teaches that the very moment (and not a moment before) one believes in and receives the Lord Jesus Christ as the Savior who died for one's sins, that person has been born (regenerated of the Spirit of God) into the family of God and has thereby become a child of God. Surely there are not two kinds of life that God freely gives to sinners: one through a special Calvinist "regeneration" and the other at salvation by faith. The eternal life received as a free gift through believing in Christ can only be the same life one receives upon being born again.

Certainly, Christ gives Nicodemus no reason to believe that the life of God received from the Holy Spirit through the new

birth differs in any way from the eternal life one receives by
faith in Him. How could "regeneration" be something else? The
fact that eternal life comes through faith and that eternal life
is only by the new birth indicates quite clearly that faith is the
requirement for and therefore precedes regeneration. Believing
in Christ unto salvation is not the *result* of regeneration but the
essential *requirement* for it to take place.

Verse after verse, in the plainest possible language, the Bible
puts believing the gospel *before* regeneration. Paul tells his children in the faith, "in Christ Jesus I have begotten you through
the gospel" (1 Corinthians 4:15), while Peter declares that we
are "born again...by the word of God...the word which by the
gospel is preached..." (1 Peter 1:23–25).

Being born again by the Word of God can refer only to
regeneration, but the Word of God is effectual only to those
who believe. Paul declares under the inspiration of God, "faith
cometh by hearing, and hearing by the word of God" (Romans
10:17) and he even calls it "the word of faith which we preach"
(verse 8). Of those who are lost, we are told that "the word
preached did not profit them, not being mixed with faith"
(Hebrews 4:2).

On the basis of abundant testimony from Scripture, we
can only conclude that faith in Christ through the gospel precedes regeneration. Therefore, the new birth does not take
place by an act of God apart from a person's understanding of
and faith in the gospel but as a result thereof. The doctrine that
one must be born again (regenerated) before one can believe is
simply not biblical.

Even Spurgeon, in spite of his claim of being a staunch
Calvinist, could not accept the teaching that regeneration came

before faith in Christ through the gospel. Calvinists quote him when he supports them, but they ignore statements such as the following:

> If I am to preach faith in Christ to a man who is regener-
> ated, then the man, being regenerated, is saved already,
> and it is an unnecessary and ridiculous thing for me to
> preach Christ to him, and bid him to believe in order
> to be saved when he is saved already, being regener-
> ate. Am I only to preach faith to those who have it?
> Absurd, indeed! Is not this waiting till the man is cured
> and then bringing him the medicine? This is preaching
> Christ to the righteous and not to sinners.[35]

Who can deny that Spurgeon's argument is both biblical and reasonable? Nor can it be denied that he was at the
same time, though unwittingly, denying the very heart of the
Calvinism he at other times stoutly affirmed.

Biblical Support for Total Depravity?

To show that the Bible does indeed teach total depravity as
inability, the Calvinist cites such scriptures as "And GOD
saw that the wickedness of man was great in the earth, and
that every imagination of the thoughts of his heart was only
evil continually" (Genesis 6:5; 8:21). Other verses offered in
alleged proof of this doctrine include Jeremiah 17:9, "The
heart is deceitful above all things, and desperately wicked," and
Romans 3:10–18, "There is none righteous...none that seeketh
after God...none that doeth good...no fear of God before their
eyes," and so forth.

Obviously, however, the fact that man's thoughts are only evil continually, that his heart is desperately wicked and deceitful, and that he neither seeks nor fears God, does not say that he is therefore *unable*, unless first of all regenerated by God, to *believe* the gospel even if convicted and convinced thereof by the Holy Spirit. Paul teaches otherwise: "ye were the servants of sin, but ye have obeyed from the heart that form of doctrine which was delivered you" (Romans 6:17). Clearly, servants of sin responded to the command to repent and believe in Christ, and as a result they were regenerated—born of the Spirit of God into the family of God, and thus saved.

Nor does the statement that "none seeks after God" deny that any man, no matter how depraved, can respond by intelligent choice without first being regenerated if God seeks and draws him. Neither does the Bible teach that God only seeks and draws an "elect" but no others. Indeed, many passages affirm that under the drawing of the Holy Spirit sinful man *can* make a moral response: "Draw me, we will run after thee" (Song of Solomon 1:4); "And ye shall seek me, and find me, when ye shall search for me with all your heart" (Jeremiah 29:13); "He [God] is a rewarder of them that diligently seek him" (Hebrews 11:6). Everyone that thirsteth, no matter how wicked, is commanded to turn unto the Lord, with never so much as a hint that this is impossible until God first regenerates them (Isaiah 55:1–7).

Furthermore, the offer of salvation is extended to "all the ends of the earth" (Isaiah 45:22). That this offer is not just for a select elect is clear. The "everyone that thirsteth" reminds one of Christ's cry, "If any man thirst, let him come unto me, and drink" (John 7:37). All those who thirst are offered the same "living water" that Christ offered to the woman at the well (John 4:10). And it is with this same promise to *whosoever will* that the Bible ends: "And whosoever will, let him take of the water of life freely" (Revelation 22:17).

The universality of God's offer of salvation is presented repeatedly throughout the Bible; for example: "preach the gospel to every creature" (Mark 16:15); and "For God so loved the world, that he gave his only begotten Son, that whosoever believeth in him should not perish, but have everlasting life" (John 3:16), etc. Surely, "every creature," "the world," and "whosoever" must include *all,* no matter how badly depraved.

It would take considerable manipulation to maintain that the offer of salvation is extended only to the elect, or even that only the elect could respond, and even then, not until they had been sovereignly regenerated. Paul confirms this desire of God for all nations when he declares to the Greek philosophers on Mars' Hill:

> God that made the world and all things therein...hath made of one blood all nations of men for to dwell on all the face of the earth, and hath determined the times before appointed, and the bounds of their habitation; That they should seek the Lord, if haply they might feel after him, and find him, though he be not far from every one of us: For in him we live, and move, and have our being; as certain also of your own poets have said.... (Acts 17:24–28)

Is it really possible that Paul's "all nations of men" and "every one of us" and "we" referred to an elect of whom the Greeks had never heard? On the contrary, Paul is clearly including his listeners and antagonists on Mars' Hill as among those who have their physical life and being from God and who may seek and find Him. This was what the Greek poets to whom he refers had said (surely these philosophers were not referring to the elect), and Paul is affirming that general understanding and declaring the person of the true God to them, a God who is "not far from every one of us," who commands all men to seek Him, and who may be found by all. There is no suggestion that anyone's depravity and bondage to sin makes it impossible to believe in Christ without first being sovereignly regenerated.

Is There a Bias at Work?

If God intends that all mankind (no matter how depraved) seek Him, and if He must be sought before He is found, then we can only conclude that those who have not yet found God and thus are not yet regenerated are capable of a genuine seeking after God as He draws *all men* unto Him (John 12:32). Calvinism's conclusion (that because of his depravity, man must be regenerated before he can believe or even seek God) is thus contrary to the clear teaching of Scripture—a fact that will be dealt with in more depth in subsequent chapters.

Calvinists often cite John 1:13 as proof that man's alleged inability due to his total depravity requires that he must first be regenerated before he can believe the gospel or receive Christ as his Savior. It speaks of those "Which were born, not of blood, nor of the will of the flesh, nor of the will of man, but of God." Commenting on this verse, Calvin writes, "Hence it follows, first, that faith does not proceed from ourselves, but is the fruit of spiritual regeneration; for the Evangelist affirms that no man can believe, unless he be begotten of God; and therefore faith is a heavenly gift."[36] In fact, Calvin's conclusion doesn't follow at all from this passage. He is reading into the text something not there in order to support his own doctrine. Indeed, he has the context backwards.

The context makes John's meaning quite clear: "He came unto his own, and his own received him not. But as many as received him, to them gave he power [the right or privilege] to become the sons of GOD, even to them that believe on his name" (verses 11–12). His own people, the Jews, rejected Christ. In contrast to those who did not receive Him, however, all those who did receive Him and believe on His name are, *as a result of receiving Him and believing*, given the right to *become* the sons of God. This new birth (verse 13) by an act of God regenerating them into His family through His Spirit is for those who have received Christ and believed "on his name" (verse 12).

Is God Sincere?

If the doctrine of Total Depravity as defined in **TULIP** were true, then from Genesis to Revelation we would have the contradiction of God pleading year after year, century after century, for repentance from a seemingly endless procession of billions of individuals who (being totally depraved) were incapable of repenting and whom He had already predestined to eternal torment from a past eternity. He would be presented in Scripture as pleading with those to repent and turn to Him whom He had created so hopelessly depraved that they could not possibly repent unless He first regenerated them, and from whom He was withholding the very regeneration and grace they needed to turn to Him, and whom He had no intention of saving. Such a scenario turns most of the Bible into a charade and mocks the rational intelligence and conscience with which God has bestowed mankind.

Yet the "moderate" Calvinist claims to affirm, in contrast to the "hyper-Calvinist," that God sincerely offers salvation to all. *Sincerely* offers salvation to those for whom Christ did not die and whom He predestined to eternal torment? This is madness. Yet Calvinists who honestly admit that the God of Calvinism does *not* love all mankind and does *not* genuinely offer salvation to all through the gospel are called "hyper-Calvinists." That label is a ploy by "moderates" to escape the horrible truth!

If because of "total depravity" man lacks the ability to respond without God's sovereign act of regeneration, then all of God's pleas are obviously both useless and senseless. There is no question that if Calvinism were true, there would be no reason for God to urge men to repent—yet He does. God's sovereign act of regeneration is alleged to require no faith or participation of any kind on man's part. Thus, the entire history of God's dealings with man as recorded in the Bible loses credibility.

Calvinism drives us into an irrational dead end. There would be no need for God to plead with the elect, whom He has already predestined to salvation, a salvation which He allegedly effects sovereignly *before* any faith is exercised on their part. Nor does it make any better sense for God to present the gospel to and plead with the non-elect who *cannot* believe it until they have been sovereignly regenerated, but whom He will not regenerate, having already damned them by His eternal decree. Yet He continues to plead and blame them for not repenting, even while He withholds from them the essential grace that He gives only to the elect! And this is only one of Calvinism's gross misrepresentations of God.

Calvin's Inconsistency

In his discussions of Total Depravity, Calvin sometimes seemed confused and unable to articulate his ideas well. He theorized that totally depraved man naturally loves truth, *but not enough*; still, he has great gifts from his Creator, and whatever truth he has comes from God—yet he cannot fully know the truth and thus be saved. One is left to wonder about the exact meaning of this terminology and where it is stated in Scripture. At other times, Calvin further contradicts himself concerning this key doctrine, and in some places even indicates that "total" doesn't *really* mean total. For example, Calvin engaged in the following confusing speculation, which seems to teeter on the brink of Total Depravity, fall over the edge at times, then recover itself:

> The human mind...is naturally influenced by the love of truth [but] this love of truth fails before it reaches the goal [yet] man's efforts are not always so utterly fruitless as not to lead to some result...and intelligence naturally implanted...should lead every individual for himself to recognize it as a special gift of God....
>
> Therefore...the human mind, however much fallen and perverted from its original integrity, is still adorned and invested with admirable gifts from its Creator.
>
> He...by the virtue of the Spirit...has been pleased to assist us...with great talents for the investigation of truth [but] not based on a solid foundation of truth....

> The Lord has bestowed on [philosophers] some slight perception of his Godhead, that they might not plead ignorance as an excuse for their impiety, and has, at times, instigated them to deliver some truths, the confession of which should be their own condemnation.... Their discernment was not such as to direct them to the truth, far less to enable them to attain it, but resembled that of the bewildered traveler....
>
> An Apostle declares, "When the Gentiles...do by nature the things contained in the law, these...shew the work of the law written in their hearts..." (Romans 2:14–15) [so] we certainly cannot say that they are altogether blind.[37]

Confusion and contradictions reign here. Is man totally depraved or isn't he? And if he is, exactly what does that mean? The belief that the natural man doesn't understand the things of God unless they are revealed to him by God cannot be denied—the Bible says so. That is true of everything we have; it all comes from God:

- He giveth to all life, and breath, and all things...for in him we live, and move, and have our being.... (Acts 17:25, 28)

- Every good gift and every perfect gift is from above, and cometh down from the Father of lights, with whom is no variableness, neither shadow of turning. (James 1:17)

But without biblical warrant, Calvin introduces the idea of degrees: All men by nature receive much truth from

God, but in varying degrees. Most of them just don't receive enough—such a quantity and quality of grace is only for the elect. Unregenerate man can see, yet he is blind—but not *totally* blind. What exactly does Calvin mean? We are left to wonder.

Faced with a Choice

Calvinists object to the assertion that the natural man is "not *so* totally depraved that he can't hear God's voice and come to Christ." They respond, "Totally depraved is totally depraved. It makes no sense to say man isn't *so* totally depraved." Not only is Total Depravity not a biblical concept, but as the quote above shows, Calvin *himself* said that man is not *so* totally depraved that he cannot receive much truth from God; he just doesn't get enough truth, because God withholds it. Why? And where does the Bible say *that?* Calvin says God withholds truth in order "to render man inexcusable...." That is like crippling a man in order to render him inexcusable for failing to run fast enough or jump high enough!

Calvin says that truth comes only from the Spirit of truth, so whatever truth man has is received from God. Then if God gives all men some truth, why doesn't He give them enough to know and seek Him? Surely God can give all mankind as much truth as He desires to give. Calvin cannot show us that man naturally has a capacity for *this* much truth but not for *that* much. How was *depravity* redefined as an *incapacity,* which isn't total but is just enough to damn the soul? There is nothing anywhere in Scripture to support such speculation.

When Peter confessed to Jesus, "Thou art the Christ," Jesus told him, "Flesh and blood hath not revealed it unto

thee, but my Father which is in heaven" (Matthew 16:15–17).
Peter must have been a totally depraved natural man when the
Father revealed Christ to him. Surely he hadn't yet been born
of the Spirit. Though he acknowledged Jesus as the Christ, he
still lacked any understanding about Christ dying for his sins.
Could not the Father, therefore, reveal Christ to everyone as He
did to Peter? Why not? Clearly, Peter had a revelation from the
Father concerning Christ *before* he was regenerated.

For all the importance Calvinism places upon the doctrine
of Total Depravity, inasmuch as that is the supposed condition
of all mankind and the elect are delivered out of it, being totally
depraved is not what keeps men in darkness after all, but God's
withholding the needed light. The lost are kept out of heaven
not only by their sin (for which there is a remedy) but by God's
withholding the grace they need for salvation, because He has
already predestined them to eternal torment—a condition
impossible to remedy!

Given what the Bible tells us of God's dealings with man
and Calvinism's doctrine of man's inability to believe, there
are only two choices: either to charge the Infinite God with
acting insincerely and in limited love and limited grace, or to
admit that Calvinism is in error. In fact, this leads to another
conclusion just as devastating to Calvinism, to be considered
in the next chapter.

1. Canons of Dort (Dordrecht, Holland, 1619), III, IV:3.

2. Garrett P. Johnson, "The Myth of Common Grace," *The Trinity Review*, March/April 1987, 1.

3. John MacArthur, Jr., *The Love of God* (Dallas, TX: Word Publishing, 1996).

4. Johnson, "Myth."

5. Cornelius Van Til, *Common Grace and the Gospel* (Phillipsburg, NJ: Presbyterian and Reformed Publishing Company, 1973), 165–66; cited in Johnson, "Myth."

6. Frank B. Beck, *The Five Points of Calvinism* (Lithgow, Australia: Covenanter Press, 2nd Australian ed., 1986), 9.

7. Dave Breese, "The Five Points of Calvinism" (self-published paper, n. d.).

8. Kenneth G. Talbot and W. Gary Crampton, *Calvinism, Hyper-Calvinism and Arminianism* (Edmonton, AB: Still Waters Revival Books, 1990), 20.

9. Edwin H. Palmer, *the five points of calvinism* (Grand Rapids, MI: Baker Books, enlarged ed., 20th prtg. 1999), 19; citing Martin Luther, *The Bondage of the Will*, trans. J. I. Packer and O. R. Johnston (Grand Rapids, MI: Fleming H. Revell, 1957), 319.

10. Ibid., 19.

11. R. C. Sproul, *Chosen by God* (Carol Stream, IL: Tyndale House Publishers, Inc., 1986), 10.

12. C. H. Spurgeon, "The Warrant of Faith" (Pasadena, TX: Pilgrim Publications, 1978), 3. One-sermon booklet from 63-volume set.

13. John MacArthur, audiotape, "The Love of God, Part 5, Romans 9" (Grace To You, 90–81, 1995).

14. John Calvin, *Institutes of the Christian Religion*, trans. Henry Beveridge (Grand Rapids, MI: Wm. B. Eerdmans Publishing Company, 1998 ed.), II: xvii, 1.

15. Spurgeon, "The Warrant of Faith," 3.

16. Calvin, *Institutes*, III: iii.

17. David J. Engelsma, "The Death of Confessional Calvinism in Scottish Presbyterianism," *The Standard Bearer*, December 1, 1992, 103.

18. David J. Engelsma, *A Defense of Calvinism as the Gospel* (The Evangelism Committee, Protestant Reformed Church, n. d.), 18.

19. Homer Hoeksema, *Reformed Dogmatics* (Grandville, MI: Reformed Free Publishing Association, 1966), 464.

20. Douglas Moo, *The Epistle to the Romans* (Grand Rapids, MI: Wm B. Eerdmans Publishing Co., 1996), 488.

21. Arthur C. Custance, *The Sovereignty of Grace* (Phillipsburg, NJ: Presbyterian and Reformed Publishing Co., 1979), 18.

22. Frederic W. Farrar, *History of Interpretation* (New York: E. P. Dutton and Co., 1886), 24.

23. John MacArthur, *The MacArthur Study Bible* (Dallas, TX: Word Publishing, 1997), 1617.

24. Palmer, *five points*, 16.

25. Quoted in *A Faith to Confess: The Baptist Confession of Faith of 1689, Rewritten in Modern English* (Carey Publications, 1986); cited in James R. White, *The Potter's Freedom* (Amityville, NY: Calvary Press Publishing, 2000), 78.

26. White, *Potter's*, 101.

27. Arthur W. Pink, *The Sovereignty of God* (Grand Rapids, MI: Baker Book House, 2nd prtg. 1986), 149.

28. J. I. Packer, "*Sola Fide:* The Reformed Doctrine of Justification" (www.the-highway.com/Justification_Packer.html).

29. Dort, Canons, III,IV:3.

30. Sproul, *Chosen*, 72.

31. Pink, *Sovereignty*, 50.

32. Westminster Confession of Faith (London: n. p., 1643), III: iii, v, vii.

33. Sproul, *Chosen*, 32.

34. C. H. Spurgeon, *Metropolitan Tabernacle Pulpit*, vol 26, 49–52.

35. C. H. Spurgeon, "The Warrant of Faith" (Pasadena, TX: Pilgrim Publications, 1978), 3. One-sermon booklet from 63–volume set.

36. John Calvin, *Commentary on the Gospel According to John* (Grand Rapids, MI: Baker Book House, 1984), 43; cited in White, *Potter's*, 182–83.

37. Calvin, *Institutes*, II: ii, 12–22.

chapter

4

"U" is for "Unconditional Election"

UNCONDITIONAL ELECTION—another phrase that is not found in the Bible—"necessarily follows from total depravity."[1] This doctrine is declared to be the heart of Calvinism. Herman Hanko writes, "No man can claim ever to be either Calvinistic or Reformed without a firm and abiding commitment to this precious truth."[2] Sproul, though a staunch Calvinist, fears that the term "can be misleading and grossly abused."[3]

The Canons of Dort explained this tenet as "the unchangeable purpose of God, whereby, before the foundation of the world, he hath out of mere grace, according to the sovereign good pleasure of his own will, chosen, from the whole human race...a certain number of persons to redemption in Christ...."[4]

Unconditional Election is the outworking of Calvinism's
extreme view of sovereignty, which allows man no freedom of
choice or action even to sin. That being the case, if anyone is
to be saved, God must choose for them. Out of Unconditional
Election, then, comes predestination to salvation.

Why so few were chosen by the God who "is love" (1
John 4:8), and the rest damned is, as we have already seen, a
major problem that Calvin himself recognized. Yet throughout
his *Institutes* he offered no satisfactory explanation. "That is
a question for which I have no answer," admitted one of the
staunchest critics of an early draft of this book. Unable to find
any place for God's love in the theory of predestination arising
out of unconditional election, Calvin struck back caustically
at his critics in his usual manner, while pleading Augustine's
authority:

> I admit that profane men lay hold of the subject of
> predestination to carp, or cavil, or snarl, or scoff. But
> if their petulance frightens us, it will be necessary to
> conceal all the principal articles of faith, because they
> and their fellows leave scarcely one of them unassailed
> with blasphemy....
>
> The truth of God is too powerful, both here and
> everywhere, to dread the slanders of the ungodly, as
> Augustine powerfully maintains.... Augustine disguises
> not that...he was often charged with preaching the doc-
> trine of predestination too freely, but, as it was easy for
> him to do, he abundantly refutes the charge....
>
> The predestination by which God adopts some to
> the hope of life, and adjudges others to eternal death...
> is greatly cavilled at, especially by those who make pre-
> science its cause.[5]

Calvin offers neither biblical nor rational proof for his (Augustine's) theory. In typical fashion, he mocks what he calls "the slanders of the ungodly" as though anyone who disagrees with him and Augustine is necessarily ungodly. Such would be his attitude toward many today who, professing a more moderate position, call themselves four-point or three-point Calvinists. As uncompromising as Calvin himself, Palmer declares,

> The first word that Calvinism suggests to most people is predestination; and if they have a modicum of theological knowledge, the other four points follow.... The Five Points of Calvinism all tie together. He who accepts one of the points will accept the other points. Unconditional election necessarily follows from total depravity." [6]

Many others agree:

> If any one of the five points of Calvinism is denied, the Reformed heritage is completely lost.... The truth of unconditional election stands at the foundation of them all [five points]. This truth is the touchstone of the Reformed faith. It is the very heart and core of the gospel. [7]

If the gospel is the power of God unto salvation to everyone who believes it (Romans 1:16), and if the five points of Calvinism comprise the very heart of the gospel, non-Calvinists cannot be saved. While many Calvinists would deny such a conclusion, it follows logically from the many statements we have already quoted by its leaders that Calvinism is the gospel and true Christianity.

Unconditional Election:
The Heart of Calvinism

The term "unconditional election" was chosen by Calvinists because it allegedly conveys the meaning that "salvation is of the Lord and not of man." Spurgeon declared, "All true theology is summed in these two short sentences: Salvation is all of the grace of God. Damnation is all of the will of man."[8] There is a confusion, however, between (1) salvation, which could only be effected through the sacrifice of Christ for our sins, and (2) our acceptance thereof, which the Bible clearly states is a *condition*: "as many as *received him*...become the sons of God" (John 1:12). Calvinists insist, however, in misguided attempts to protect their extreme view of God's sovereignty, that salvation cannot be conditioned upon any act or belief on man's part. George L. Bryson rightly states:

> Calvinistic Election says to the unregenerate elect, "Don't worry, your Depravity is no obstacle to salvation," and to the unelect, "Too bad, you have not been predestined for salvation but [to] damnation."[9]

R. C. Sproul writes, "The term *election* refers specifically to one aspect of divine predestination. God's choosing of certain individuals to be saved."[10] Sproul continues, "The Reformed view teaches that God positively or actively intervenes in the lives of the elect to ensure their salvation."[11]

Man's acceptance or rejection of Christ plays no part: "By making election conditional upon something that man does, even if what he does is simply to repent and believe the gospel,

God's grace is seriously compromised."[12] How the acceptance of God's grace by faith can compromise that grace is not explained, nor could it be. Paul declares that God's grace is received by faith alone (Ephesians 2:8). But Calvinism rejects faith as essential to regeneration and thus to salvation.

The Calvinist insists that God must "intervene" sovereignly to "regenerate" the elect without their having any faith in Christ or understanding of the gospel. Indeed, "faith" is declared to be a "work." "To reject [Calvinistic] election is to reject salvation by grace and promote salvation by works."[13] Thus by the erroneous view that faith is a work, the very faith God requires is denied as the means by which God's grace is received by man!

In the Bible, however, faith and works are contrasted as opposites. "By grace are ye saved, through faith;...not of works" (Ephesians 2:8–9); "But to him that worketh not, but believeth..." (Romans 4:5). To support Calvinism, the Bible must be contradicted in many places.

Calvinism's Unbiblical View of Sovereignty—AGAIN

Unconditional Election is demanded by the distorted view of God's sovereignty, which we have earlier discussed and which undergirds all of Calvinism: that every thought, word, and deed is decreed by God—including all sin. We have already shown that this perspective is both irrational and unbiblical, but to the Calvinist it is a major foundation of his belief: "The all-out emphasis on the almighty sovereignty of Jehovah God is the truth and beauty of Calvinism."[14] Another writer adds, "Only the Calvinist...recognizes God's absolute sovereignty."[15]

On the contrary, all Christians believe that God is absolutely sovereign, but many recognize that sovereignty is not incompatible with freedom of choice. God is no less sovereign because Satan and mankind have rebelled and disobey Him continually.

Palmer declares with no apparent sense of contradiction that "God...has foreordained...even sin."[16] In fact, sin is rebellion against God, so it could hardly be willed by Him. Nevertheless, like Palmer, Gordon H. Clark insists that

> ...every event is foreordained because God is omniscient.... Of everything God says, 'Thus it must be....' Must not they who say that God does not foreordain evil acts now hang their heads in shame?[17]

Clark, Palmer, Pink, et al., are simply echoing Calvin, who said that God "foresees the things which are to happen, simply because he has decreed that they are so to happen...." How, then, can Calvinists today deny that Calvinism teaches that God causes sin? As we have noted, Calvin goes on to reason that it is therefore "vain to debate about prescience, while it is clear that all events take place by his [God's] sovereign appointment."[18] Following their leader, many Calvinists argue, "If a single event can happen outside of God's sovereignty, then He is not totally sovereign, and we cannot be assured that His plan for the ages will be accomplished."[19]

This theory, as we have seen, cannot be found in Scripture, nor is it reasonable. Deliverance from this false view comes by simply recognizing that there is a vast difference between what

God decrees and what He allows, between what God desires and what His creatures do in disobedience of His will and rejection of His love. John R. Cross, who made the revealing New Tribes Mission video, *Delivered from the Power of Darkness*, has said it well:

> From the third chapter of Genesis on, the scriptures shout "free will." The whole volume talks about choices, and the associated consequences. God saw fit to write an entire book on choices, the Book of Wisdom (Proverbs). Having a free will makes sense of God's free love....
>
> Suppose you met someone who...showed real love for you—going out of his way to do special things for you...telling you they loved you. Then you found out that they had no choice—they were programmed to "be loving"...well, it would be a terrible disappointment. It would all seem so artificial, so meaningless, so empty. And it would be.
>
> Man was given a choice.... Having this choice defined man as a human being: to eat or not to eat, to obey or disobey, to love or not to love. Man was not a robot. Man was able to love by his own free choice [without which love is not love].[20]

Does God Cause Man to Sin?

It is true that God, being omniscient, knows all before it happens, and therefore nothing can happen that He doesn't know. For the omniscient God to know all, however, it is clearly not necessary that He must *decree and cause* all. Yet Calvin, limiting foreknowledge, insisted that God knows only what He has decreed; therefore, for God to know all, He must be the cause of all, including all evil. The doctrine of Unconditional Election then follows: that just as evil is God's doing, so election, too, must be all of God without even faith on man's part. Pink readily confesses the logical conclusion to which Calvinism's view of sovereignty and omniscience ultimately lead:

> ...to deny God's foreknowledge is to deny His omniscience.... But we must go further: not only...did His omniscient eye see Adam eating of the forbidden fruit, but He *decreed* beforehand that he *should* do so. (Emphasis in original) [21]

On the contrary, we have already seen that God, being separate from the time-space-matter universe He created, observes it from outside of time; thus His foreknowledge of the future leaves man free to choose. For God there is no time. Past, present, and future are meaningful only to man as part of his temporary existence in this physical universe.

God's knowledge of what to Him is one eternal present would have no effect upon what to man is still future. Calvin himself accepted this view without realizing its devastating impact upon his denial of man's ability to make genuine choices:

> When we ascribe prescience to God, we mean...that to his knowledge there is no past or future, but all things are present, and indeed so present, that...he truly sees and contemplates them as actually under his immediate inspection. [22]

Are "Tempting" and "Testing" Meaningless Terms?

Calvinism reasons that God, having foreordained from eternity past that Adam and Eve would eat of the Tree of Knowledge, forbids them to eat of it so He can punish them for doing what He foreordained and caused them to do! Then, by Unconditional Election, He saves a select number of their descendants to show His grace. That incredible scenario is contrary to the very character of a holy and just God who "cannot be tempted with evil, neither tempteth he any man" (James 1:13). Far from *causing* sin, God doesn't even *tempt* man to sin, as we have already seen.

We have noted that the Hebrew word translated "tempt" is *nacah*. It means to test or prove, not to entice to sin. When God asked Abraham to sacrifice Isaac, He was not enticing Abraham to commit murder but was testing Abraham's faith and obedience. To suggest that Abraham's every thought, word, and deed had already been foreordained by God makes any "test" of Abraham's faith meaningless. The same would be true of the hundreds of times God tested the faith and obedience of individuals and nations in the Bible.

Peter declares that the testing "of your faith [is] much more precious than of gold" (1 Peter 1:7). How can he speak of "*your* faith" if faith is all of God? And how can there be any meaningful "test" if man has no will and all has been predetermined by God from eternity past?

God gave Adam and Eve the easiest possible command. There must have been hundreds if not thousands of trees in the Garden bearing delicious fruit of many kinds. They could eat of any or all of them—except one: "Of every tree of the garden thou mayest freely eat: but of the tree of the knowledge of good and evil, thou shalt not eat of it: for in the day that thou eatest thereof, thou shalt surely die" (Genesis 2:16–17). This command was a necessary test of obedience and of love for their Creator.

God was *testing,* not *tempting,* His creatures. But this whole concept of warning man not to tempt God, and God testing man's obedience and faith, which occupies so many pages of Scripture, is meaningless if all has been eternally foreordained by God. This doctrine makes a mockery of all of God's pleadings through His prophets for man to repent, and renders the gospel itself redundant. Why plead with or warn or preach to those whose response has been foreordained from eternity past?

Incapable and Predestined, Yet Accountable?

According to the "T" in TULIP, man is unable to respond to God in any way except rebellion. He is free to pursue sin and to reject the gospel, but because he is totally incapable of seeking or pleasing God by the Calvinist definition, he cannot believe the gospel or have any faith in God. He can respond to God only in unbelief and disobedience. Palmer declares that "the non-Christian is hostile to God...he is not even able to understand the good."[23] White says he can understand but not embrace it.

Allegedly, by His eternal decree God has predestined man's every thought, word, and deed, including the most heinous atrocities committed by the world's worst criminals. Man's rebellion is only the acting out of what God has predetermined man will and must do—so man isn't a rebel but a puppet.

How can that which God foreordained and causes man to do be condemned as sinful rebellion against God's will? How can it be disobedience to do what God has willed? How could God complain when man does what He predestined him to do? And how could man then be justly punished for doing what he has no capability of *not* doing?

Such doctrine defames the God of love and justice who reveals Himself to mankind in the Scriptures. In defense of the character of the true God, John Wesley argued reasonably and biblically:

> He [God] will punish no man for doing anything he could not possibly avoid; neither for omitting anything which he could not possibly do. Every punishment supposes the offender might have avoided the offence for which he is punished. Otherwise, to punish him would be palpably unjust, and inconsistent with the character of God....[24]

Astonishingly, Calvinists see neither injustice nor contradiction in God foreordaining man's sin and then punishing him for what he could not avoid doing. This extreme view of sovereignty and predestination is applied to salvation by the doctrine of Unconditional Election. Although the Bible declares clearly and repeatedly that faith is the condition for salvation ("believe...and thou shalt be saved...he that believeth not shall be damned," etc.), Calvinism's Unconditional Election will not even allow faith unto salvation. God simply decides to save some, called "the elect," sovereignly regenerates them, and only thereafter gives them faith to believe on Christ, and damns the rest by His eternal decree. And God allegedly foreordains all this before He brings the doomed and damned into existence.

Scripture and conscience, however, impose upon *man* the duty to rescue everyone possible. But the Calvinist insists that it glorifies God for *Him* to rescue only a limited "elect." John MacArthur calls the elect "those chosen by God for salvation...."[25] That He chooses to damn the rest is said to show how wonderful it was that He saved at least some, thus causing the elect to be exceedingly grateful. The Calvinist attempts to escape the question of why God who *is love* saves so few by saying that the real wonder is that God would save *any*—which is no answer at all.

By this doctrine, if anyone is to be saved God must, through Irresistible Grace (which we will come to later), sovereignly *effect* within the sinner a saving response to the offer of salvation. Clark admitted, "The two theses most unacceptable to the Arminians are that God is the cause of sin and that God is the cause of salvation...."[26] Referring to the pronouncement of this doctrine at the Synod of Dort, England's King James (who gave us the King James Bible), though he was no Arminian and hardly a "saint," expressed his repugnance:

> This doctrine is so horrible, that I am persuaded, if there were a council of unclean spirits assembled in hell, and their prince the devil were to [ask] their opinion about the most likely means of stirring up the hatred of men against God their Maker; nothing could be invented by them that would be more efficacious for

this purpose, or that could put a greater affront upon
God's love for mankind than that infamous decree of
the late Synod....[27]

A Strained and Unwarranted Redefinition of Words

Who could argue with the king's condemnation? Nevertheless,
the attempt is made to muster biblical support by redefining
certain words and phrases, such as "world," "whosoever,"
"any," "all men," and even "sinners" to mean only the elect.
For example, Paul's statement that "Christ Jesus came into
the world to save sinners" (1 Timothy 1:15) seems on its face
to mean that His desire was for all sinners to be saved. That
understanding would, of course, refute Calvinism. Therefore,
the word "sinners" is redefined to mean only "the elect among
sinners."

There is nothing anywhere in the Bible, however, to suggest that "sinners" really means the elect. The words "sinner"
and "sinners" are found nearly seventy times in the Bible: "the
men of Sodom were wicked and sinners" (Genesis 13:13); "the
wealth of the sinner is laid up for the just" (Proverbs 13:22);
"behold, the Son of man is betrayed into the hands of sinners" (Mark 14:41); "for sinners also love those that love them"
(Luke 6:32); "we know that this man is a sinner" (John 9:24);
"we know that God heareth not sinners" (John 9:31); "the law
is not made for a righteous man, but for...the ungodly and
for sinners" (1 Timothy 1:9); "but this man [Christ]...is holy,
harmless, undefiled, separate from sinners" (Hebrews 7:24–
26), etc. There is not one place in the Bible where "sinners"

could be construed to mean "the elect."

Yet when the salvation of sinners, or God's love for sinners, is spoken of, then the Calvinist insists that "sinners" means the elect, such as in the following statements: "I am not come to call the righteous, but sinners to repentance" (Matthew 11:19; Luke 7:34), "This man receiveth sinners" (Luke 15:2); "while we were yet sinners, Christ died for us" (Romans 5:8), and so forth. Such redefinitions are required all through Scripture in order to support Calvinism.

Throughout the New Testament, the same Greek word is always used for "sinners." Thus there is no license whatsoever to give it a different meaning in certain cases in order to rescue Calvinism. Clearly, Calvinism would collapse if the Bible really meant that Christ came to save *all* sinners without discrimination, instead of only *some* sinners, i.e., the elect among them.

Who Are the Elect, and Why?

The Bible uses the term "elect" in a variety of ways: for Israel, Christ, a lady, a church, and angels. Never, however, is this word used to indicate that there is a select group who alone have been predestined to be saved. *Never*. Ironside declared, "Nowhere in the Bible are people ever predestinated to go to hell, and nowhere are people simply predestinated to go to Heaven... predestination is always to some special place of blessing." [28]

Calvinism defines the elect as that select group whom, alone, God has from eternity past appointed to salvation. All others are predestined by God to eternal damnation. The gospel can be preached day and night to the latter, yet to no avail, because they are totally incapable of believing it. God allegedly has no desire whatsoever to open their blind eyes and give them the faith to believe. He does that for the elect alone (through Unconditional Election), though He could do so for all. Yet *never* is this repugnant doctrine taught in Scripture!

"Moderate" Calvinists would claim that we have just described hyper-Calvinism. Attempting to deny "reprobation" or "double-predestination" (which Calvin clearly taught), the moderates would say that God merely left the non-elect to the just consequences of their sin. Left to their doom those He *could have rescued*, or predestined them to that fate—what is the difference? The so-called "hyper-Calvinist" simply admits the truth about Calvinism.

What "moderates" try to distance themselves from as "hyper" was taught by Calvin and has been part of mainstream Calvinism from the beginning. The Westminster Confession of Faith states, "By the decree of God, for the manifestation of His own glory, some men and angels are predestinated unto everlasting life, and others foreordained to everlasting death."[29] Yet having taught this belief, Calvin admitted:

> …many…deem it most incongruous that of the great body of mankind some should be predestinated to salvation and others to destruction.[30]
>
> The decree, I admit, is dreadful; and yet it is impossible to deny that God foreknew what the end of man was to be before he made him, and foreknew, because he had so ordained by his decree.[31]

Calvin is forced to maintain what he admits is a "dreadful" decree. Why? Not by Scripture but by his unbiblical insistence that God can only foreknow what He decrees. From that error, it follows that since God knows everything that will occur, He must have decreed everything that would ever happen—from Adam's fall to the final doom of billions. Thank God that the Bible says the opposite: that "God so loved the *world,* that he gave his only begotten Son, that *whosoever* believeth in him should not perish, but have eternal life" (John 3:16; emphases added). Both "world" and "whosoever" must be changed to "elect" for Calvinism to be sustained.

Perplexing Indeed!

Calvinism's "elect" are unconditionally (i.e., without any faith, understanding or choice on their part) elected to salvation simply because, in the mystery of His sovereign will, God decided, for no reason at all, to save them and *only* them. The Calvinist objects when we say, "for no reason at all." It is claimed that God needs no reason, that it simply pleased Him so to do, or that the reason is hidden in the mystery of His will: "We do not know what God bases His choice on...."[32]

Even God, however, must have a reason for saving some and damning others. Otherwise He would be acting unreasonably, and thus contrary to His Being. In fact, election/predestination is always said in the Bible to result from God's foreknowledge.[33] Those *whom He foreknew would believe* He predestined to special blessings, which He decided would accompany salvation from sin's penalty—"the things which God hath prepared for them that love him" (1 Corinthians 2:9).

God continually explains why man is separated from Him and what the solution is, and He offers to reason with man about this matter: "Come now, and let us reason together" (Isaiah 1:18). He reasons with Israel, sends His prophets to warn His chosen people, and explains repeatedly why, though reluctantly, He punishes them: "because of the wickedness of thy doings" (Deuteronomy 28:20); "they have forsaken the covenant of the LORD" (Deuteronomy 29:25); "because they have forsaken my law" (Jeremiah 9:13), etc. God explains that He gave His Son to die for the sins of the world because of His great love for all mankind: "For God sent not his Son into the world to condemn the world; but that the world through him might be saved" (John 3:17); "And we have seen and do testify that the Father sent the Son to be the Saviour of the world" (1 John 4:14).

Yet God never declares in Scripture a reason for saving a select group and damning all others. Surely such an important doctrine would be clearly explained, in defense of God's character, yet it isn't even mentioned. We can only conclude that Unconditional Election is but a human invention.

Scripture and Conscience Are United Against It

In fact, man's God-given conscience and Scripture cry out in protest against this doctrine. God is entirely "without partiality" (James 3:17), is "no respecter of persons" (Acts 10:34), and all men are equally worthy of His condemnation and equally unworthy of His grace. Calvinists admit that the "elect," like all mankind by their view, were once totally depraved, incurably set against God and incapable of believing the gospel, with no more to commend them to God's grace than the "non-elect." Then why did He select them to salvation and damn all the rest?

No reason can be found either in God or in man, or anywhere in Scripture.

There is no escaping the haunting question: Why did Calvin's God choose to save so few when He could have saved all? Without apology, James White informs us, "Why is one man raised to eternal life and another left to eternal destruction...? It is 'according to the kind intention of His will.'"[34] So it is God's *kindness* that causes Him to save so few and to damn so many! We are aghast at such a concept, and we are offended on behalf of our God.

Biblically, there is no question that God has the right to save whom He will and no one could complain. We are all deserving of the eternal punishment required by God's holiness against sin. But we are repeatedly told that God *is love* and that He is merciful to *all*, exactly what we would expect of Him in view of His command to us to love our neighbors as ourselves and to do good to all. We surely would not expect the "Father of mercies, and the God of all comfort" (2 Corinthians 1:3) to withhold mercy from *any* who so desperately need it— much less that He would take pleasure in doing so. Calvin hides behind Augustine's authority to justify this contradiction, but the effort falls short. For example:

> Now...he [God] arranges all things by his sovereign counsel, in such a way that individuals are born, who are doomed from the womb to certain death, and are to glorify him by their destruction.... If your mind is troubled, decline not to embrace the counsel of Augustine....[35]
>
> We admit that the guilt is common, but we say, that God in mercy succours some. Let him (they say) succour all. We object, that it is right for him to show

by punishing that he is a just judge.... Here the words of Augustine most admirably apply.... Since God inflicts due punishment on those whom he reprobates, and bestows unmerited favour on those whom he calls, he is free from every accusation....[36]

I will not hesitate...to confess with Augustine that the will of God is necessity...[and] that the destruction consequent upon predestination is also most just.... The first man fell because the Lord deemed it meet that he should...because he saw that his own glory would thereby be displayed....[37]

What "Justice" Is This?

God does not resort to judgment in order to demonstrate that He is a just judge. He *is* perfectly just, and His judgment falls upon those who deserve it and who reject His pardon through Christ—not upon a vast multitude whom He predestines to eternal torment because it pleases and glorifies Him! That belief of Calvin and Augustine libels the God of the Bible.

That God would impose "the necessity of sinning" upon man, then condemn him for sinning, cannot be called "just" by any semantic maneuver. Yet this is exactly what Calvin taught and defended:

> The [predestined to damnation] reprobate would excuse their sins...because a necessity of this nature is laid upon them by the ordination of God. We deny that they can thus be validly excused...every evil which they bear is inflicted by the most just judgment of God.[38]

The heartlessness that Calvin attributes to God is appalling.

Surely, as Wesley argues, to punish for failure to do what it is impossible to do, or for having done what one could only do, is the opposite of justice. If that were not bad enough, that God would predestine man to sin so that He would have someone to judge is abhorrent even to the ungodly. It is offensive to the conscience God has given all mankind. Calvin attributes evil to God, then calls it just because "everything which he [God] wills must be held to be righteous."[39]

Scripture tells us the opposite—that God commands all men to repent, pleads with mankind to do so, is ready to pardon and promises salvation to all who believe on Christ. The following passages, in which God pleads with mankind to accept the salvation He offers in Christ, are only a few among many similar scriptures that refute Calvinism's Unconditional Election:

> Let the wicked forsake his way, and the unrighteous man his thoughts: and let him return unto the LORD, and he will have mercy upon him; and to our God, for he will abundantly pardon (Isaiah 55:7); Ye shall seek me and find me, when ye shall search for me with all your heart" (Jeremiah 29:13); Therefore, whosoever heareth these sayings of mine, and doeth them, I will liken him unto a wise man, which built his house upon a rock (Matthew 7:24); Come unto me, all ye that labour and are heavy laden, and I will give you rest (Matthew 11:28); If any man thirst, let him come unto me, and drink (John 7:37); And whosoever will, let him take the water of life freely (Revelation 22:17).

Each of the above very clearly includes two facts that refute Unconditional Election:

1) The command and invitation are given to all, not just to a select group. The words "wicked" and "unrighteous" and "whosoever" and "all" clearly mean what they say and cannot be turned into "elect."

2) There are conditions that must be met. There is both a command and an invitation to meet certain requirements: to "forsake" one's sin, to seek God with the whole heart, to "hear and do" what Christ commands, to "come" to Him, and to "take and drink" the water of life that Christ gives.

Evading the Issues

In all of his talk about God's sovereignty and justice, Calvin takes no account of God's other attributes such as His love and mercy. Not once in the nearly 1,300 pages of his *Institutes* does Calvin expound upon God's love for mankind or attempt to explain how God, who *is* love, could take pleasure in damning billions whom He could save if He so desired. How, indeed! Here is the great question that the very conscience God has implanted in all mankind finds so troubling—but Calvin never addresses it!

Biblically, God's sovereignty is exercised only in perfect unity with His total character. He is not a despotic sovereign. His sovereignty is enforced in harmony with His love, grace, mercy, kindness, justice and truth—but Calvin has almost nothing to say about these attributes, because they cannot be reconciled with his theory.

It is only reasonable to ask why God, who *is love*, lacks the love and compassion to save all whom He could save, and

instead predestines billions to eternal torment. Calvin repeatedly hides his lack of an answer behind the word "mystery." But
pleading "mystery" cannot cover up the horror of this doctrine.
Yet that is the best Calvin can do, along with repeatedly appealing to Augustine's authority. He argues:

> Let us not be ashamed to be ignorant in a matter in
> which ignorance is learning. Rather let us willingly
> abstain from the search after knowledge, to which it is
> both foolish as well as perilous, and even fatal to aspire.[40]
>
> How sinful it is to insist on knowing the causes
> of the divine will, since it is itself, and justly ought to
> be, the cause of all that exists.... God, whose pleasure
> it is to inflict punishment on fools and transgressors...
> no other cause can be adduced...than the secret counsel
> of God.... Ignorance of things which we are not able,
> or which it is not lawful to know, is learning, while the
> desire to know them is a species of madness.[41]

Pleading "mystery" and exalting ignorance is contrary to
God's Word, which tells us that we must "be ready always to
give an answer to every man that asketh you a *reason*..." (1 Peter
3:15). Yet Calvin said it was wrong to seek a reason.

The only Greek word translated "mystery" is *musterion*.
It is *never* used as Calvin used it to denote a secret not to be
revealed. Rather, it *always* refers to knowledge that is being
revealed. For example: "I would not...that ye should be ignorant
of this mystery..." (Romans 11:25); "I shew you a mystery..."
(1 Corinthians 15:51); "made known unto me the mystery..."
(Ephesians 3:3); "Even the mystery which hath been hid...but
now is made manifest..." (Colossians 1:26); "I will tell thee the
mystery..." (Revelation 17:7), etc. The word is *never* used as

Calvin uses it in relation to salvation, predestination, or sovereignty, and certainly not concerning some being saved and others damned.

No Escape by Semantics

According to the doctrine of Unconditional Election, both the faith to believe and the salvation the elect receive are imposed upon them by God's sovereignty, overriding entirely their alleged human incapacity to choose and their depraved will's rejection of the gospel. The Calvinist objects to the phrase "imposed upon them" and insists that God simply removed from the elect their natural resistance to the gospel.

Any removal, however, of the alleged natural rejection would have to change a rebellious sinner's desire. Palmer admits, "He even *makes* me, who really did not love Jesus, want to love Him and believe in Him (emphasis added)."[42] On the contrary, no one can be *made* either to love or to accept a gift, much less to change his mind without the willingness to do so. That willingness must come from the heart; it can't be created out of thin air.

No one can be forced to change his mind. No matter how he attempts to explain Unconditional Election, the Calvinist cannot escape a basic fact recognized by all mankind: that in any meaningful change of attitude or belief, the human will must consent for reasons that it accepts willingly. But that commonsense fact undermines God's sovereignty, according to Calvinism. On the contrary, it is a fact, and it refutes Calvinism.

The Calvinist claims that, according to Ephesians 2:8–10, faith is bestowed as a gift (we discuss that error in depth later).

The Greek construction, however, demands that salvation, not faith, is the gift of God. Moreover, even if faith were the gift, it would have to be received—an act in itself requiring faith and the exercise of one's will. Saving faith is an absolutely essential element in any relationship and transaction between man and God, as many scriptures declare unequivocally: "He that *cometh* to God must *believe* that he is..." (Hebrews 11:6; emphases added).

Jesus said, "According to *your* faith be it unto you" (Matthew 9:29). We have already pointed this out, but it bears repeating. The expression "your faith" is found twenty-four times: "your faith is spoken of..." (Romans 1:8); "if Christ be not raised, your faith is vain... (1 Corinthians 15:17), etc. "Thy faith" is found eleven times: "thy faith hath made thee whole..." (Mark 5:34; Luke 8:48); "the communication of thy faith..." (Philemon 6), etc. "His faith" is found twice: ("his faith is counted for righteousness" (Romans 4:5), etc., and "their faith" three times: "Jesus saw their faith" (Mark 2:5), etc. These are odd expressions if no one can have faith unless God sovereignly regenerates him—then gives him a faith that is not his own but totally of God.

Such teaching is clearly not biblical. Scripture repeatedly depicts God as appealing to man's reason, conscience, and will in order to persuade him to repent and believe. The entire history of God's dealing with man—past, present, and future, as revealed in Scripture—is a meaningless charade if Unconditional Election is true. And so it is with all of TULIP.

In Summary

It is love's essential ingredient—the power of choice—that Calvinism's misguided defense of a false view of God's sovereignty will not allow. And it is right here on Unconditional Election, the second of its five points, that Calvinism stubs its toe again on a huge contradiction over which its adherents cannot agree. Its perversion of sovereignty demands that whether one goes to heaven or hell depends solely upon God's will and decree; a man's receiving or rejecting Christ is not by his free choice but is irresistibly imposed upon him by God. As a result, the atheist feels justified in rejecting a God who, contrary to basic human compassion, predestines multitudes to eternal torment whom He could just as well have predestined to eternal joy in His presence.

Why wouldn't the God who *is love* exercise the absolute control Calvinism attributes to Him over every thought, word, and deed to eliminate sin, disease, suffering, and death and to bring all mankind into heaven? This contradiction of the basic standards that God has put in every human conscience raises an obvious question—and it is a question in response to which Calvinists themselves cannot agree upon an answer.

Some, like John Calvin, unashamedly say that God doesn't want everyone saved—indeed, that it is his "good pleasure" to damn so many. Others, realizing the revulsion that idea creates in anyone with a normal sense of mercy and kindness, call this "hyper-Calvinism" and attempt to find other explanations for God's alleged failure to irresistibly elect everyone. The necessity to overcome non-Calvinists' objections to God's apparent callousness (in predestining multitudes to eternal torment before they were even born) has been the mother of invention to a number of attempted rationalizations.

As we have seen, some try to escape the moral disaster by simply saying that the answer is hidden in the secret of God's will—an obvious copout. Others, while admitting the monstrous contradiction, insist that what to us seems abhorrent is not so to God—that we cannot impose our standards upon Him. That argument, however, is demolished by the fact that God has written His standards in every conscience and reasons with mankind upon that very basis (Isaiah 1:10–20).

All through Scripture, God appeals to man's conscience to do what he knows is right and to refrain from evil. Christ's teaching, "And as ye would that men should do to you, do ye also to them likewise" (Luke 6:31), clearly expresses the common sympathy that every normal person, though a sinner, realizes he ought to have for those in need. That this compassion comes from God and reflects His own kind desire toward mankind cannot be denied, and is acknowledged to be so by Spurgeon.

Calvinists cannot agree on how to handle Paul's clear declaration that God desires "all men to be saved" (1 Timothy 2:4). As we shall see later in more detail, like James White, many Calvinists argue that Paul doesn't mean "all men" but "all classes of men."[43] Calvin himself adopted this devious idea for escaping the truth concerning God's love for all.[44] Yet Spurgeon rejected this ploy. Instead, he honestly declared (as we have already noted):

> As it is my wish that it should be so, as it is your wish that it might be so, so it is God's wish that all men should be saved; for assuredly, he is not less benevolent than we are.[45]

This un-Calvinistic belief, however, got Spurgeon in trouble. Wasn't he contradicting the Limited Atonement he otherwise professed to accept? How could God sincerely wish for the salvation of those for whom Christ did not die and whom He had predestined to everlasting torment? And here—like Sproul, Piper, MacArthur, and others—Spurgeon fell back upon the idea that God apparently has two wills, "God's will of decree (His eternal purpose)…[and] God's will of desire."[46]

This sermon is apparently the origin of MacArthur's assertion of the same contradiction. How could God have two conflicting wills? Instead of finding a biblical and rational solution to this unbiblical and irrational idea (which must be maintained in order to defend Calvinism), Spurgeon pleaded ignorance:

> Then comes the question, "But if he wishes it to be so, why does he not make it so…[God] has an infinite benevolence which, nevertheless, is not in all points worked out by his infinite omnipotence; and if anybody asked me why it is not, I cannot tell. I have never set out to be an explainer of all difficulties, and I have no desire to do so."[47]

In fact, Calvinism itself creates this "difficulty"! The dilemma dissolves and the unanswerable question is answered by one simple admission: God in His sovereignty has given man the genuine power of choice. Thus God's sincere and loving desire for all mankind to be saved is not contradicted by His justice but is rejected by the free will of many. No one is *predestined* either to eternal bliss in God's presence or to eternal torment in separation from Him. Eternal destiny depends upon one's acceptance or rejection of Christ through the gospel.

Those who receive Christ have nothing to glory in but in Christ alone who paid the penalty for their sins. And those who suffer the just penalty for their sins have only themselves to blame for having willfully rejected the salvation God graciously provided and freely offered as a gift of His love.

Such is the clear teaching of Scripture from Genesis to Revelation. But to face that fact, the Calvinist would have to abandon the dogmas to which he has devoted his life and reputation. Many have done so. It is our prayer that this book will help many more to be delivered from TULIP.

1. Edwin H. Palmer, *the five points of calvinism* (Grand Rapids, MI: Baker Books, enlarged ed., 20th prtg., 1999), 27.

2. Herman Hanko, Homer C. Hoeksema, and Gise J. Van Baren, *The Five Points of Calvinism* (Grand Rapids, MI: Reformed Free Publishing Association, 1976), 28.

3. R. C. Sproul, *Chosen by God* (Carol Stream, IL: Tyndale House Publishers, Inc., 1986), 155.

4. Canons of Dort (Dordrecht, Holland, 1619), 1:7.

5. John Calvin, *Institutes of the Christian Religion*, trans. Henry Beveridge (Grand Rapids, MI: Wm. Eerdmans Publishing Company, 1998 ed.), III: xxi, 4,5.

6. Palmer, foreword to *five points*, 27.

7. Herman Hanko; cited in Laurence M. Vance, *The Other Side of Calvinism* (Pensacola, FL: Vance Publications, rev. ed. 1999), 245.

8. Charles Haddon Spurgeon, *Spurgeon at His Best*, ed. Tom Carter (Grand Rapids, MI: Baker Book House, 1988), 122.

9. George L. Bryson, *The Five Points of Calvinism "Weighed and Found Wanting"* (Costa Mesa, CA: The Word For Today, 1996), 36.

10. R. C. Sproul, *Grace Unknown* (Grand Rapids, MI: Baker Books, 1997), 141.

11. Sproul, *Chosen*, 142.

12. C. Samuel Storms, *Chosen for Life* (Grand Rapids, MI: Baker Book House, 1987), 55.

13. Carl Morton, in *The Berea Baptist Banner*, January 5, 1995, 19.

14. David J. Engelsma, *Hyper-Calvinism and the Call of the Gospel* (Grandville, MI: Reformed Free Publishing Association, 1980), 133.

15. Leonard J. Coppes, *Are Five Points Enough? The Ten Points of Calvinism* (Denver CO: self-published, 1980), 15.

16. Palmer, *five points*, 25.

17. Gordon H. Clark, *Predestination* (Phillipsburg, PA: Presbyterian and Reformed Publishing Co., 1987), 63–64; cited in Vance, *Other Side*, 265.

18. Calvin, *Institutes*, III: xxiii, 6.

19. Calvinist pastor in Arizona to Dave Hunt, August 11, 2000. On file.

20. John R. Cross, *The Stranger on the Road to Emmaus* (Olds, AB: Good Seed International, 1997), 56–57.

21. Arthur W. Pink, *The Sovereignty of God* (Grand Rapids, MI: Baker Book House, 2nd prtg. 1986), 249.

22. Calvin, *Institutes*, III: xxi, 5.

23. Palmer, *five points*, 15.

24. In Vance, *Other Side*, 236.

25. John MacArthur, *The MacArthur Study Bible* (Nashville, TN: Word Publishing, 1997), 1939.

26. Clark, *Predestination*, 185.

27. King James I; in Jacobus Arminius, *The Works of James Arminius*, trans. James and William Nichols (Grand Rapids, MI: Baker Book House, 1986), 1:213.

28. H. A. Ironside, *In the Heavenlies, Addresses on Ephesians* (Neptune, NJ: Loizeaux Brothers, 1937), 34.

29. Westminster Confession of Faith (London: 1643), III:3.

30. Calvin, *Institutes*, III: xxi, 1.

31. Calvin, *Institutes*, III: xxiii, 7.

32. Palmer, *five points*, 26.

33. See, for example, Romans 8:29 and 1 Peter 1:2.

34. James R. White, *The Potter's Freedom* (Amityville, NY: Calvary Press Publishing, 2000), 177.

35. Calvin, *Institutes*, III: xxiii, 5,6.

36. Ibid., 11.

37. Ibid., 8,9.

38. Ibid.

39. Ibid., 2.

40. Ibid., xxi, 2.

41. Ibid., xxiii, 4,8.

42. Palmer, *five points*, 21.

43. James R. White, *The Potter's Freedom* (Amityville, NY: Calvary Press Publishing, 2000), 139–143.

44. John Calvin, *Calvin's New Testament Commentaries* (Grand Rapids, MI: Wm. B. Eerdman's Publishing Co., 1994), 10:209.

45. C. H. Spurgeon, sermon preached January 16, 1880, "Salvation by Knowing the Truth," [www.apibs.org/chs/1516.htm].

46. Ibid.

47. Ibid.

"L" is for "Limited Atonement"

THE "L" IN TULIP represents one more integral theory in Calvin's scheme of salvation: "the doctrine which limits the atonement to...the elect."[1] This concept follows directly from the limitation Calvinists place upon God's love in spite of the fact that it, like every facet of His Being, is infinite. One of their prominent apologists declares, "The Bible teaches again and again that God does not love all people with the same love...'loved by God' is not applied to the world but only to the saints...(Romans 1:7)."[2]

Same love? But love is love—and "love...is kind" (1 Corinthians 13:4). Calvin himself declared, "All are not created on equal terms, but some are preordained to eternal life, others to eternal damnation...."[3] Is it loving or kind to "preordain to... eternal damnation"? Again we ask, *What Love Is This?*

A. A. Hodge confesses: "If they [critics] could prove that

the love which prompted God to give his Son to die, as a sin offering...had for its objects all men...that Christ actually sacrificed his life with the purpose of saving all...on the condition of faith, then...the central principle of Arminianism is true [and Calvinism is false]...."[4] Boettner explained further:

> The Reformed Faith has held to the existence of an eternal, divine decree which, antecedently to any difference or desert in men themselves separates the human race into two portions and ordains one to everlasting life and the other to everlasting death.... Thus predestined and foreordained...their number is so certain and definite that it cannot be either increased or decreased.[5]

We protest that this doctrine is an outrageous misrepresentation of God. The God-given conscience of every person, saved and unsaved, recoils at the thought of creating beings simply in order to predestine them to eternal torment! Tragically, Calvinism forces its adherents to reject the normal human compassion that is otherwise held in common with all mankind.

Carson draws the line at Limited Atonement, arguing that this label "is singularly unfortunate for two reasons. *First*, it is a defensive, restrictive expression: here is atonement, and then someone wants to limit it. The notion of limiting something as glorious as the Atonement is intrinsically offensive. *Second*, even when inspected more coolly, 'limited atonement' is objectively misleading. Every view of the Atonement 'limits' it in some way, save for the unqualified universalist."[6]

His last sentence is a common Calvinist error—which accuses even those who say Christ died for all—of limiting the efficacy of the atonement because only those who believe are saved. On the contrary, the atonement is not limited by some rejecting Christ's sacrifice on their behalf. The inheritance left by the deceased is not reduced in value because some heirs refuse their share.

Honoring God's Love Is Heresy?

To the Calvinist, as Stanley Gower, a member of the Westminster Assembly, declared, there is no greater heresy than the suggestion that "God loveth all alike, Cain as well as Abel, Judas as the rest of the apostles."[7] Thus one must explain away that verse familiar to every Sunday-school child, "For God so loved the world, that he gave his only begotten Son, that whosoever believeth in him should not perish, but have everlasting life" (John 3:16). For Calvinism to stand, this verse (and many others expressing the same truth) cannot mean what the words seem to say: "world" and "whosoever" cannot signify all mankind but only the elect. Thus Calvinist children mean something else if ever they sing, "Jesus loves the little children, all the children of the world...." He only loves *some* of the children of the world!

Sproul writes, "The world for whom Christ died cannot mean the entire human family. It must refer to the universality of the elect (people from every tribe and nation)."[8] John Owen boldly states, "That the *world* here cannot signify all that ever were or should be, is as manifest as if it were written with the beams of the sun...."[9] How odd, then, that this bright sun is visible only to Calvinists—and that they disagree with one another on this key doctrine.

John MacArthur defends "The Love of God to Humanity."[10] He quotes Calvin that "the Father loves the human race,"[11] and that in John 3:16, God "useth the universal note [world] both that He may invite all men in general unto the participation of life, and that He may cut off all excuse from unbelievers." [12] But how can God invite "unto the participation of life" those whom He has predestined to eternal death in the Lake of Fire—and how can God "cut off all excuse from unbelievers," if Christ didn't die for them, and they were predestined to eternal torment from a past eternity? This is double talk!

MacArthur uses "humanity" in the generic sense, attempting thereby to deny God's love for every individual. Calvinists insist that God has a different kind of love for the elect than for the non-elect. [13] But love is love—and love of no kind predestines anyone to eternal torment who could be saved.

Calvinism's limitation upon the atonement of Christ ignores Old Testament types of the Cross, undermines the gospel, and limits God's boundless love. Owen, "after a more than seven years' serious inquiry...into the mind of God about these things..." asked earnestly, "To what purpose serves then general ransom [i.e., the alleged "heresy" that Christ loves all and died for all], but only to assert that Almighty God would have the precious blood of his dear Son poured out for innumerable souls whom he will not have to share in any drop thereof, and so, in respect of them, to be spilt in vain, or else to be shed for them only that they might be the deeper damned?" [14]

But it is Calvinism's predestination to damnation that creates this contradiction. Notice Owen's phrase, "whom he will not have to share in any drop thereof...." Of course it would be senseless for Christ to die for any whom God had determined to exclude from salvation. God did not exclude anyone. It is *man* who has rejected the salvation Christ provided for *all*.

No less sincere and earnestly concerned for truth, H. A. Ironside expressed the opposing common evangelical understanding in contrast to Calvinism's limited atonement for only a select number:

> No matter how far they [any sinners] have drifted from God; no matter what their sins may be, they do not have to peer into the book of the divine decrees in order to find out whether or not they are of the chosen or the elect. If they come in all their sin and guilt, confessing their iniquities and trusting in Christ, then they may have the assurance from His Word that they are saved. It has been well said that the "Whosoever *wills* are the elect, and the whosoever *won'ts* are the non-elect."[15]

Calvinists, however, firmly follow Calvin, who said of God, "for, (as he hates sin) he can only love those whom he justifies [i.e., the elect]."[16] Gerstner argues that if John 3:16 "is supposed to teach that God so loved everyone in the world that He gave His only son to provide them an opportunity to be saved by faith...such love on God's part...would be a refinement of cruelty.... Offering a gift of life to a spiritual corpse, a brilliant sunset to a blind man, and a reward to a legless cripple if only he will come and get it, are horrible mockeries."[17]

We agree that it would be cruel mockery to offer salvation to those whom God had no intention of saving and would not help to respond to the offer. But who says that all mankind cannot respond, if they so desire? Not the Bible, which offers salvation to "whosoever will," but Calvinism, which effectively changes "whosoever" into "elect"! So this "cruelty" is imposed by Calvinism itself, beginning with the very first of its five points. Yet "moderates," blaming all on "hyper-Calvinists," claim to believe that God sincerely loves and offers salvation to all, while in the same breath they say Christ did not die for all.[18]

By defining "total depravity" as "total inability," Calvinism says that none can respond to the gospel, not even the elect, until they have been sovereignly regenerated. Yet Christ commanded the gospel to be preached to everyone—and no one warns the non-elect that it isn't for them. Of course, how could they be warned, since no one knows who they are? So Christ commanded "cruelty and mockery"? And the Calvinist engages in it each time he preaches the gospel!

Why preach salvation to those already predestined to eternal damnation? "We must," says the Calvinist, "because no one knows who are the elect." So there is no escaping the fact that if Calvinism is true, then it is a cruel mockery to preach the gospel to anyone except the elect—but there is no way to identify them.

Would it lessen the non-elect's pain for the evangelist to explain, "This good news is only for the elect, so disregard it if you are not among them"? No, that would only add to the confusion. The cruelty is inherent in Calvinism's misrepresentation of God and His gospel.

The Doctrine Clearly Stated

Where does Scripture say that Christ's blood cannot be shed for those who would not benefit thereby? Nowhere. But this fiction is foundational to the doctrine of Limited Atonement: "that the cross of Christ provides a sure, secure and real salvation for everyone God intended it to save and for them alone."[19] Homer Hoeksema confesses the dire consequences of this belief, "If Christ died for the elect only, then there are no possible benefits in that death of Christ for anyone else...."[20] Steele and Thomas insist,

> Christ's redeeming work was intended to save the elect only and actually secured salvation for...certain specified sinners.... The gift of faith is infallibly applied by the Spirit to all for whom Christ died, thereby guaranteeing their salvation.[21]

This doctrine, however, is nowhere stated in the entire Bible in plain words, but is required by the rest of TULIP. Michael Horton argues, "If Jesus died for every person, but not every person is saved, His death did not actually save anybody.... If Christ died for people who will be in hell, His efforts cannot accurately be called a 'saving work' [and] there is no real saving power in the blood. Rather, the power would seem to be in the will of the creature."[22]

On the contrary, man's will has no power but can only accept or reject the salvation God offers in the gospel. The Calvinist complaint is like saying that the $1 million, which a father deposits in a bank in his estranged son's name, is of no value unless the son accepts it. Obviously, the sinner's acceptance of Christ no more gives the blood of Christ saving power than the son's acceptance of the $1 million would give it monetary value.

With no clear statement in all of Scripture to support this dogma, it must be defended by rationalizations: "If Christ died for all men and all men are not saved, the cross of Christ is of no effect. Calvary is a sham."[23] Of course, that doesn't follow. Otherwise, giving the Ten Commandments was a sham, because all men do not keep them.

Even Sproul acknowledges that "the value of Christ's atonement is sufficient to cover the sins of the world...." [24] It would have to be, because His perfect sacrifice must be of infinite value. Although "the cross is to them that perish foolishness" (1 Corinthians 1:18), it is not a sham but saves all who believe! As one of the most respected Bible teachers of recent years said, "The Bible teaches most strongly the doctrine of unlimited atonement.... The doctrine of limited atonement is specifically denied in Scripture...." [25]

But Calvinists persist: "Only Calvinism with its effective atonement limits man's power and exalts God's power and glory." [26] On the contrary, God offers salvation on His terms. That multitudes reject His offer only sends them to hell—hardly anything of which they could boast! Those who reject Christ are no more "in charge" than the multitudes who daily break God's commandments. Were Adam and Eve "in charge" when they rebelled? Was Satan? Of course not!

Did their rebellion give "power" to Satan, and to Adam and Eve? Of course not! Nor did it (any more than man's continued rebellion today) take anything away, in even the slightest degree, from either God's power or His glory. The Calvinist is driven to such fallacious and unbiblical arguments in his desperation to defend an indefensible dogma.

While some who call themselves Calvinists reject Limited Atonement, it is irrational to do so while accepting the other four points. A leading Calvinist author writes: "It is in this truth of limited atonement that the doctrine of sovereign election (and, in fact, sovereign predestination with its two aspects of election and reprobation), comes into focus." [27] In other words, the whole Calvinistic system collapses if Limited Atonement is not biblical, which indeed it is not.

Key, Yet Controversial — Even Among Calvinists

Limited Atonement is the one point that even Calvinists find difficult to accept. Certainly Spurgeon, at times, contradicted that which at other times he affirmed.

The book of Hebrews makes it clear that the Levitical system God gave to Israel for dealing with sin, involving the tabernacle, temple, priests and offerings, was "a figure for the time then present" (Hebrews 9:9), which pointed to the sacrifice of Christ that was to come. Indisputably, the Old Testament provision for sin and salvation was for *all Israel*, not for a special elect among them. Disobedience and unbelief were the only barriers separating every Israelite from God's grace. For example: "And the priests...made reconciliation... upon the altar...for *all Israel*...the burnt offering and the sin offering...for *all Israel*" (2 Chronicles 29:24); "offered burnt offerings...for *all Israel*" (Ezra 8:35); "the law of Moses...which I commanded...for *all Israel*, with the statutes and judgments" (Malachi 4:4), etc. (emphases added).

Spurgeon was accused of "Arminianism" for urging all unsaved to come to Christ, which he habitually did with great earnestness, thus contradicting Calvinism's claim that the number of those for whom Christ died was fixed and limited. Nor did he refrain from criticizing those whom he classified as hyper-Calvinists for their rejection of what was then called "duty-faith," meaning that it was the duty of all men to repent and believe the gospel.

It was over his persistent preaching of this message, in spite of much criticism, that the "duty-faith controversy" raged among "particular Baptists" in England. Spurgeon declared: "I cannot imagine a more ready instrument in the hands of Satan for the ruin of souls than a minister who tells sinners that it is not their duty to repent of their sins or to believe in Christ, and who has the arrogance to call himself a gospel minister, while he teaches that God hates some men infinitely and unchangeably for no reason whatever but simply because he chooses to do so." [28]

Spurgeon is criticizing the very heart of Calvinism—no wonder there was a furor! Many Calvinists of his day considered such statements to be a denial of Limited Atonement—which indeed they are. For pointing this out, I have been accused of misquoting and misrepresenting Spurgeon.

Some consider the doctrine of Limited Atonement to be "the Achilles Heel of Calvinism." [29] On the other hand, some Calvinists consider it to be their strongest point, "the hardest one of the *'Five Points of Calvinism'* for Arminians to cope with." [30] Most admit that it follows necessarily from Calvinism's view of predestination/reprobation: "If God has elected some and not others to eternal life, then plainly the primary purpose of Christ's work was to redeem the elect." [31]

We agree that it would be unreasonable for Christ to die for those whom God had from eternity past predestined to eternal torment, if there were such. But that problem is created by Calvinism's five points. "Give up this point [Calvinist election]," says another Calvinist, "and we have lost the battle on the sovereignty of God in salvation."[32]

The Calvinist recognizes that Unconditional Election and Limited Atonement "must stand or fall together. We cannot logically accept one and reject the other."[33] But the Bible repeatedly declares that Christ died for all mankind, that the gospel is offered and equally available to all, and that God wants all to be saved. Definitions of words must be changed to deny this clear biblical teaching.

Even John MacArthur acknowledges that God *desires* all men to be saved—but then he says that God inexplicably doesn't elect and predestine to salvation multitudes of those He desires to be saved. Odd, indeed, considering the emphasis Calvinists put on sovereignty, that God doesn't sovereignly fulfill His own desire![34]

Hodges notes that the God of Limited Atonement "is hardly the God of love whom we meet in the Bible. The deity of the determinist creates human beings for whom he has no direct love, and who have no free will, and thus they are created solely for…everlasting torment. Christ's death in no way affects them, and so they stand totally outside of any redemptive provision." He goes on to argue:

> The cruelty implicit in such a view is obvious to any observer outside of those who have been brought up in, or have bought into, this kind of theology. Despite specious arguments addressed to every text alleged against such theology, determinists of this type are bereft of true biblical support. It is absurd, for example, to claim (as they sometimes do) that when the Bible says, "God so loved the world," it means only "the world of the elect."[35]

In considering the scriptures bearing on this subject, it becomes clear that the only way Limited Atonement can be defended is to assign, arbitrarily, a restrictive Calvinist meaning to key words. Palmer boldly declares:

> It was just because God so loved the world of elect sinners that He sent His only begotten Son that the world [i.e., the elect by Calvinist definition] might be saved through Him (John 3:16–17). In this passage, "world" does not mean every single person, reprobate as well as elect, but the whole world in the sense of people [elected] from every tribe and nation....[36]

What evidence is there, either within this passage and its context or anywhere else in Scripture, that "world" has this restrictive Calvinist meaning? Palmer offers none, nor is there any.

Why Aren't All Men Saved?

In maintaining Limited Atonement, the Calvinist reasons, "If Christ paid the debt of sin, has saved, ransomed, given His life for *all* men, then *all* men will be saved."[37] In the same vein, Palmer writes, "But if the death of Jesus is what the Bible says it is—a substitutionary sacrifice for sins...whereby the sinner is really reconciled to God—then, obviously, it cannot be for every man...for then everybody would be saved, and obviously they are not."[38]

In a letter to John Wesley, George Whitefield reasoned, "You cannot make good the assertion 'that Christ died for them that perish,' without holding...'that all the damned souls would hereafter be brought out of hell....'" [39] This argument, however, rests upon the unbiblical theory that Christ's death immediately saved all of the elect, without any faith, understanding, or acceptance on their part. Contradicting many fellow Calvinists, Pink admitted, "A Saviour *provided* is not sufficient: he must be *received*. There must be '*faith* in His blood' (Romans 3:25) and faith is a *personal* thing. *I* must exercise faith." [40]

Though criticized by other Calvinists as an extremist on this point, Pink was right. That Christ "taste[d] death for every man" (Hebrews 2:9) does not automatically mean that all are delivered from eternal death, the penalty for sin. Nowhere does the Bible say so. Sinners are invited and urged to *come* to Christ and to *believe* on Him. Such is the sinner's responsibility—something he "*must*...do to be saved" (Acts 16:30).

That Christ died for our sins is the message preached in the gospel. It must, however, be believed to be of benefit to a sinner. Christ's death, though offered for "all men," is only efficacious for those who believe: He is "the Saviour of all men, specially of those that believe" (1 Timothy 4:10). Vance points out the obvious problem if the death of Christ automatically procures salvation for those for whom He died:

> But if the nature of the atonement was such that it actually in and of itself provided salvation for those for whom it was intended, then the "elect" could never have been born "dead in trespasses and sins" (Ephesians 2:1). And consequently, how could men who were saved, redeemed, reconciled, and justified be "by nature children of wrath" (Ephesians 2:3)...? [41]

The Passover, which Pink acknowledges as "one of the most striking and blessed foreshadowments of the Cross-work of Christ to be found anywhere in the Old Testament, is a clear example of the principle that the Atonement and its application are to be distinguished. The blood of the slain Passover lamb (Exodus 12:6,21) became efficacious only after it was applied to the doorpost per instructions (Exodus 12:7,22).... The death of the lamb saved no one: the blood had to be applied."[42] And so it is with Christ's death.

Calvinism bluntly blames God: "Because God has loved certain ones and not all, because He has sovereignly and immutably determined that these particular ones will be saved, He sent His Son to die for them, to save them, and not all the world."[43] Thus, all men are not saved because God doesn't want them to be and has predestined multitudes to suffer eternally.

According to the Bible, however, all are not saved because *they* (the lost) refuse to believe on Christ. Paul writes that salvation comes "unto all...that believe...for all have sinned" (Romans 3:22–23). Surely the "all have sinned" means all mankind. Thus the "all...that believe" must mean that all mankind *may* believe on Christ, if they will.

Salvation Is for All

Here are some of the many verses (with key words and phrases italicized) that declare that God (exactly as we would expect of the One who *is love* and the Father of mercies) loves everyone with *infinite* love and desires that *all* should be saved. He does not want anyone to perish and has made the death of Christ propitiatory for the sins of all mankind if they will only believe on Him:

- *All* we like sheep have gone astray; we have turned every one to his own way; and the Lord hath laid on him the iniquity of us all. (Isaiah 53:6) [Surely the "all" who went astray are the same "all" (i.e., all Israel and all mankind) whose iniquity was laid upon Christ.]

- Behold the Lamb of God, which taketh away the sin of *the world*." (John 1:29) [Just as the Old Testament sacrifices were offered for all Israel and not for a select group of Israelites, so the fulfillment thereof in Christ's sacrifice as the Lamb of God was offered for the whole world of mankind and not for a limited "elect."]

- And as Moses lifted up the serpent in the wilderness, even so must the Son of man be lifted up: that *whosoever believeth* in him should not perish, but have eternal life. For God so loved *the world*, that he gave his only begotten Son, that *whosoever believeth* in him should not perish.... [F]or God sent not his Son into *the world* to condemn *the world;* but that *the world* through him might be saved. *He that believeth* on him is not condemned.... *He that believeth* on the Son hath everlasting life: and *he that believeth not* the Son shall not see life.... (John 3:14–18, 36) [Healing via the upraised serpent of brass, which Christ said pictured His being lifted up on the Cross, was for *all* who would look in faith.]

- Remember ye the law of Moses...which I commanded...for *all Israel*.... (Malachi 4:4) [The law, with its accompanying sacrifices, was for *all* Israel—and the fulfillment in Christ is for *all* mankind.]

- If *any man* thirst, let him come unto me, and drink.... (John 7:37)

- For I am not ashamed of the gospel of Christ: for *it is the power of God unto salvation to every one that believeth*; to the Jew first, and also to the Greek. (Romans 1:16)

- Christ died for *the ungodly*. (Romans 5:6) [*All* are ungodly, not only the elect.]

- But the scripture hath concluded *all* under sin, that the promise by faith...might be given to *them that believe*. (Galatians 3:22)

- For the wages of sin is death; but the *gift of God* is eternal life through Jesus Christ our Lord. (Romans 6:23)

- Christ Jesus came into the world *to save sinners*. (1 Timothy 1:15) [Surely the elect are not the only sinners.]

- Who will have *all men* to be saved, and to come to the knowledge of the truth. (1 Timothy 2:4)

- Who gave himself a ransom *for all*.... (1 Timothy 2:6)

- We trust in the living God, who is the *Saviour of all men*, specially of those that *believe*. (1 Timothy 4:10)

- That he by the grace of God should taste death *for every man*. (Hebrews 2:9)

- The Lord is...not willing that *any* should perish, but that *all* should come to repentance. (2 Peter 3:9)

- If we confess our sins, he is faithful and just to forgive us our sins, and to cleanse us from all unrighteousness.... And if *any man* sin, we have an advocate with the Father, Jesus Christ the righteous: And he is the propitiation for our sins: and *not for ours only; but also for the sins of the whole world*. (1 John 1:9–2:2)

- The Father sent the Son to be the *Saviour of the world*. (1 John 4:14)

To take these many (and the many others similar) clear declarations that salvation is for *all*, for the *world*, for *whosoever*, for *all Israel*, for *any man*, for *every one that believeth*, etc., and dare to say that only an elect group is in mind is to deliberately change God's Word!

Do only the elect go astray like lost sheep? Do only the elect thirst? Are only the elect ungodly and sinners? Are only the elect "under sin"? Obviously not. As surely as all men are sinners and have, like all of Israel, gone astray like lost sheep, so surely were the sins of all men laid upon Christ, and salvation is available to all through faith in Him.

These verses, and many more like them, clearly state in unambiguous language that Christ was sent to be "the Saviour of the world," that His death was "a ransom for all" and that He is therefore "the Saviour of all men" who will but believe. John Owen attempts to counter such scriptures and to support Limited Atonement with the following commentary upon 1 Timothy 1:15, "Christ Jesus came into the world to save sinners":

> Now, if you will ask who these sinners are towards whom he hath this gracious intent and purpose, himself tells you, Matthew 20:28, that he came to "give his life a ransom for *many*;" in other places called *us* believers distinguished from the world: for he "gave himself for *our* sins, that he might deliver *us* from this present evil *world*..." Galatians 1:4.... Ephesians 5:25–27, "He loved the church, and gave himself for *it*...." Titus 2:14,

"He gave himself for *us*, that he might redeem *us* from
all iniquity..." for through him "*we* have access into the
grace wherein we stand," Romans 5:2, etc.[44]

An Unwarranted Assumption

Owen was brilliant, yet his argument is fallacious. His desire to
defend Calvinism seemingly blinded him to the Scriptures and
to simple reason. Obviously, the multitude of verses that state
clearly that God loves all and is merciful to all and that Christ
died for all are not nullified by other verses declaring that Christ
died for the *church*, that His death was a ransom for *many*, or
the assurance that He died for *us*, etc. These passages do not
say that Christ died *only* for *many* sinners, *only* for the *church*,
only for *us*, etc. By that interpretation, statements such as, "For
if through the offense of one [Adam] many be dead...by one
man's disobedience many were made sinners" (Romans 5:15,
19), etc., would indicate that only a limited number were made
sinners and died through Adam's disobedience.

Of course, the apostles, writing to believers, would remind
them that Christ died for *them*—but that statement cannot
void the many clear declarations that He died for all. Yet this
same argument is offered repeatedly by Calvinists to this day.
Piper quotes the same inapplicable verses in which it is said that
Christ was "a ransom for many," that He "bare the sin of many,"
and that He "loved the church and gave himself for her," etc. as
"proof" that Christ's death was not propitiatory for all.[45]

By such reasoning, Paul wouldn't have been able to use
"you," "ye," etc., in writing to the Corinthians because that
would mean the benefits of Christ's death and resurrection

were *only for them*. By the same argument, for David to say, "The LORD is *my* shepherd..." (Psalm 23:1) would mean that this was true only for David. Or when Israel's prophets wrote, "O God of *Israel*, the Saviour...their redeemer is strong, the LORD of hosts is his name..." (Isaiah 45:15; Jeremiah 50:34), it meant that God was the God and redeemer only of Israel.

Equally absurd, for Paul to say "the Son of God who loved *me*" (Galatians 2:20) would mean that Christ loved only Paul. Other arguments that Calvinists employ are equally unreasonable. Consider the following attempt by John Piper and his pastoral staff to explain away 1 Timothy 4:10:

> Christ's death so clearly demonstrates God's just abhorrence of sin that he is free to treat the world with mercy without compromising his righteousness. *In this sense* Christ is the savior of *all* men. But he is *especially* the Savior of those who believe. He did not die for all men in the same sense.... The death of Christ actually saves from *all* evil those for whom Christ died "especially."[46] [Emphasis in original]

Sense or Nonsense?

Can anyone make sense of "Christ did not die for all men in the *same* sense," yet He is the savior of all men "in *this* sense"? What is *this* sense? Because Christ's death "demonstrates God's just abhorrence of sin..." He is able to "treat the world with mercy without compromising his righteousness." But He doesn't treat all with mercy, because Christ "did not die for all men in the same sense...." Neither *this sense* nor *same sense* are defined, so we can't make *any sense* out of this nonsense. But it shows again the lengths to which one must go to defend Calvinism.

One is reminded of Spurgeon's objection (we've quoted it several times because it so clearly contradicts the Calvinism he otherwise affirmed) to such attempts to get around the clear words of Scripture. In commenting upon 1 Timothy 2:4 (contradicting his own defense of Limited Atonement at other times), he said:

> I was reading just now the exposition of [one] who explains the text so as to explain it away [as] if it read "Who will not have all men to be saved...." [In fact,] the passage should run thus—"whose wish it is that all men should be saved...." As it is my wish...as it is your wish...so it is God's wish that all men should be saved; for, assuredly, he is not less benevolent than we are.[47]

Yet Spurgeon contradicted himself again in saying that God is able to save all He desires to save. Since all are not saved, God's wish that all men should be saved cannot be sincere. Consequently, He *is* less benevolent than Spurgeon, who desired all men to be saved—and surely less benevolent than Paul, who was willing to be "accursed from Christ" if that would save his brethren the Jews (Romans 9:1–5). How could God desire all men to be saved, be able to save all He desires to save, yet all are not saved?

As we have just seen, John MacArthur, Jr. (like Spurgeon) tries to escape the obvious contradiction by saying that God has a "will of decree" and a "will of desire."[48] In the process of escaping one contradiction, he falls into another. How could God, given Calvinism's extreme view of sovereignty, fail to decree anything He truly desires? Calvinists boast that they exegete Scripture. But where in I Timothy 2:4 (or anywhere else) is there even a hint of "two wills," one of "decree" and one of "desire" as Piper and others also teach?

It is the imposition upon Scripture of an unbiblical theory that entraps the Calvinist in such contradictions. Obviously, the contradiction would disappear if free will were admitted—but that cannot be allowed, because it would destroy TULIP.

Boettner declares that "Calvinists hold that in the intention and secret plan of God, Christ died for the elect only...."[49] Otherwise, adds Boettner, "If Christ's death was intended to save all men, then we must say that God was either unable or unwilling to carry out His plans."[50] He forgets that Christ's death only benefits those who *receive* Christ (John 1:12) and that salvation, being "the gift of God" (Romans 6:23), must be willingly received. As for men being able to oppose God's plans, is the evil in the world God's plan? Why, then, are we to pray, "Thy will be done, on earth as it is in heaven"?

Remember Isaiah is speaking to all of Israel when he says, "all we like sheep have gone astray..." and when he declares that "the iniquity of us all" would be laid upon the coming Messiah. As surely as all went astray, so surely did God lay upon Christ the iniquity of *all*—yet many Israelites throughout history have not been saved. These and many other scriptures make it clear that the benefit of Christ's death, burial, and resurrection in full payment for the sins of the world is available to be received by whosoever believes the gospel, while the wrath of God abides upon all who reject Christ and the salvation genuinely offered to all in Him.

1. John Murray, *Redemption Accomplished and Applied* (Grand Rapids, MI: Wm B. Eerdmans Publishing Co., 1955), 64.

2. Edwin H. Palmer, *the five points of calvinism* (Grand Rapids, MI: Baker Books, enlarged ed., 20th prtg. 1999), 44.

3. John Calvin, *Institutes of the Christian Religion*, trans. Henry Beveridge (Grand Rapids, MI: Wm. Eerdmans Publishing Company, 1998 ed.), III: xxi, 5.

4. A. A. Hodge, *The Atonement* (Memphis, TN: Footstool Publishers, 1987), 348.

5. Loraine Boettner, *The Reformed Doctrine of Predestination* (Phillipsburg, NJ: Presbyterian and Reformed Publishing Co., 1932), 83–84.

6. D. A. Carson, *The Difficult Doctrine of the Love of God* (Wheaton, IL: Crossway Books, 2000), 73.

7. Stanley Gower, in the first of "Two Attestations" to John Owen, Bk. 1 of *The Death of Death in the Death of Christ* (n. p., 1647); in *The Works of John Owen*, ed. William H. Goold (Carlisle, PA: The Banner of Truth Trust, 3rd prtg. 1978), X:147.

8. R. C. Sproul, *Chosen by God* (Carol Stream, IL: Tyndale House Publishers, Inc., 1986), 207.

9. Gower, in *Owen, Works*, IV:338.

10. John MacArthur, Jr., *The Love of God* (Dallas, TX: Word Publishing, 1996), xv 85–86, 99–124.

11. John Calvin, *Commentary on a Harmony of the Evangelists, Matthew, Mark, and Luke*, William Pringle, trans. (Grand Rapids, MI: Baker, 1930), 314, cited in MacArthur, *Love of God*, 85.

12. MacArthur, *Love of God*, 195.

13. Ibid., 12–18.

14. Owen, *Works*, I:149.

15. H. A. Ironside, *Timothy, Titus and Philemon* (Neptune, NJ: Loizeaux Brothers, Inc., 1990), 55.

16. Calvin, *Institutes*, III: xi, 11.

17. John H. Gerstner, *Wrongly Dividing the Word of Truth: A Critique of Dispensationalism* (Brentwood, TN: Wolgemuth and Hyatt, Publishers, Inc., 1991), 124.

18. MacArthur, *Love of God*, 106–112.

19. Grover E. Gunn, *The Doctrine of Grace* (Memphis, TN: Footstool Publications), 1987, 17.

20. Cited in Laurence M. Vance, *The Other Side of Calvinism* (Pensacola, FL: Vance Publications, rev. ed. 1999), 423.

21. David N. Steele and Curtis C. Thomas, *The Five Points of Calvinism* (Phillipsburg, NJ: Presbyterian and Reformed Publishing Co., 1963), 17.

22. Michael Scott Horton, *Putting Amazing Back Into Grace* (Nashville, TN: Thomas Nelson Publishers, 1991), 89.

23. Herman Hanko, *God's Everlasting Covenant of Grace* (Grandville, MI: Reformed Free Publishing Association, 1988), 15.

24. R. C. Sproul, *Grace Unknown* (Grand Rapids, MI: Baker Books, 1997), 165.

25. Dave Breese, "The Five Points of Calvinism" (self-published paper, n. d.).

26. Leonard J. Coppes, *Are Five Points Enough? The Ten Points of Calvinism* (Denver CO: self-published, 1980), 49.

27. Homer Hoeksema, *Limited Atonement*, 151; cited in Vance, *Other Side*, 406.

28. C. H. Spurgeon, *New Park Street Pulpit* (London: Passmore and Alabaster), Vol 6, 28-29; sermon preached December 11, 1859.

29. Kenneth G. Talbot and W. Gary Crampton, *Calvinism, Hyper-Calvinism and Arminianism* (Edmonton, AB: Still Waters Revival Books, 1990), 11.

30. Ibid., 37.

31. Boettner, *Reformed*, 151.

32. Joseph M. Wilson, "How is the Atonement Limited?" *The Baptist Examiner*, December 9, 1989.

33. Boettner, *Reformed*, 151.

34. John MacArthur, *The MacArthur Study Bible* (Nashville: Word Publishing, 1997) 1862.

35. Zane C. Hodges, "The New Puritanism, Pt. 3: Michael S. Horton: Holy War With Unholy Weapons," *Journal of the Grace Evangelical Society,* Spring 1994, 7:12, 17–29.

36. Palmer, *five points*, 44–45.

37. W. J. Seaton, *The Five Points of Calvinism* (Carlisle, PA: The Banner of Truth Trust, 1970), 15.

38. Palmer, *five points*, 44.

39. Cited in Vance, *Other Side*, 423.

40. Arthur W. Pink, *Gleanings in Exodus* (Chicago: Moody Press, 1981), 84.

41. Vance, *Other Side*, 427.

42. Pink, *Gleanings*, 88.

43. Palmer, *five points*, 50.

44. Owen, *Works*, 1:157–58.

45. John Piper and Pastoral Staff, "TULIP: What We Believe about the Five Points of Calvinism: Position Paper of the Pastoral Staff" (Minneapolis, MN: Desiring God Ministries, 1997), 16–17.

46. Ibid., 14–15.

47. C. H. Spurgeon, *Metropolitan Tabernacle Pulpit*, vol. 26, "Salvation by Knowing the Truth," sermon preached on 1 Timothy 2:3–4, January 16, 1880.

48. John MacArthur, *The MacArthur Study Bible* (Nashville, TN: Word Publishing, 1997), 1862.

49. Boettner, *Reformed*, 150.

50. Ibid., 155.

chapter

6

"I" is for "Irresistible Grace"

IN THE DOCTRINE of Irresistible Grace, we find once again the pervasive influence of Augustine. Boettner informs us, "This cardinal truth of Christianity [Irresistible Grace] was first clearly seen by Augustine."[1] Warfield says Augustine "recovered [it] for the Church."[2] Likewise, some Baptists agree that "Augustine may be regarded as the father of the soteriological system [called] 'Calvinism.'"[3] Sproul even says, "Augustinianism is presently called Calvinism or Reformed Theology."[4] Shedd declares:

> Augustine accounts for the fact that some men are renewed and some are not, by the unconditional decree (*decretum absolutum*), according to which God determines to select from the fallen mass of mankind (*massa perditionis*), the whole of whom are alike guilty and under condemnation, a portion upon whom he bestows renewing grace, and to leave the remainder to their own self-will and the operation of law and justice.[5]

Having once taught free will and that God desired to save all mankind,[6] Augustine later changed his view. Faith became something that God irresistibly bestowed upon the elect without their having believed anything or having made any decision or even having been aware that they were being regenerated.[7] By such reasoning, man (being by nature dead in sin) can't even *hear* the gospel—much less respond to the pleadings of Christ. Irresistible Grace is necessitated by this unbiblical premise, to which Calvinists cling in spite of the fact that our Lord calls to *all*, "Come unto me, *all* ye that labour and are heavy laden, and I will give you rest.... If *any* man thirst, let him come unto me, and drink" (Matthew 11:28; John 7:37), etc. (emphases added). Apparently *all*, even the spiritually dead, can hear and come and drink, as other passages make very clear. Dave Breese writes, "If grace were irresistible, one fails to understand even the reason for preaching the gospel...."[8] Certainly, it would be absurd for God to plead with men to repent and believe, if they *cannot* unless He irresistably causes them to do so.

The Serious Consequences of Sovereignty Misapplied

To recap Calvinism up to this point: because of Total Depravity, those whom God has unconditionally elected and predestined to eternal life and for whom alone Christ died are first sovereignly regenerated without faith, understanding, or even knowing it is happening to them. Thereafter (some would say simultaneously) the grace to believe on Christ as Savior and Lord is irresistibly imposed upon the newly regenerated elect, whom God from eternity past has predetermined to save, and they are given faith to believe on Christ. Piper says that man must first

> ...be born of God. Then, with the new nature of God, he immediately receives Christ. The two acts (regeneration and faith) are so closely connected that in experience we cannot distinguish them...new birth is the effect of irresistible grace...an act of sovereign creation....[9]

Irresistible Grace is essential in the Calvinist theory of salvation. No one can resist God's saving grace, irresistibly imposed upon those whom He has predestined to eternal life. As Piper says, "[T]here can be no salvation without the reality of irresistible grace. If we are dead in our sins, totally unable to submit to God, then we will never believe in Christ unless God overcomes our rebellion."[10]

Sadly, this doctrine, too—like all of TULIP—leads to a denial of God's love, mercy, and grace as revealed in Scripture. Piper declares, "God is sovereign and can overcome all resistance when he wills...irresistible grace refers to the sovereign work of God to overcome the rebellion of our hearts and bring us to faith in Christ so that we can be saved."[11] If that were true, God could have irresistibly imposed grace upon Adam and Eve and spared mankind the suffering and evil that resulted from their rebellion. Why didn't He? *What love is this?*

Does God actually love and have compassion not for the world (as the Bible says) but for a limited elect only (as Calvinists insist)? Piper says God chose to save the elect alone by irresistibly imposing His grace upon them and He predestined

the remainder of mankind to eternal torment. Isn't such a sce-
nario abhorrent to every conscience? And doesn't it malign the
God of the Bible, whose "tender mercies are over all his works"
(Psalm 145:9) and who "would have all men to be saved" (1
Timothy 2:4)?

If, as the Bible declares, God truly loves all and has given
them the power of choice, then the lost are responsible for their
own doom through willfully rejecting the salvation God lov-
ingly and freely offers in Christ. Yet Hodge declares, "According
to the Augustinian scheme, the non-elect have all the advantages and opportunities of securing their salvation...." [12] What
advantages and opportunities for salvation do those have from
whom God withholds the regeneration and irresistible grace
without which Calvinists say no one can believe unto salvation,
for whom Christ didn't die, and whom He predestined to eternal doom before they were born? This is mockery! Yet Sproul,
Piper, MacArthur, and other leading "moderate" Calvinists of
today persist in this obvious contradiction!

Furthermore, how can such persons be justly held accountable? Should a paraplegic be faulted for failing to become a
world-class gymnast, or a man for failing to bear children or to
breastfeed the children his wife bears? Absurd! Yet we are told
that God's perfect justice operates in this fashion. Tragically,
Calvinism's misrepresentation of God has caused many to turn
away from God as from a monster.

Allegedly, God has created all men incapable of choosing
to seek Him and of believing the gospel. The only hope is in
God himself sovereignly regenerating the sinner—but He only
does this for a limited elect and damns the rest in order to prove
His sovereignty and justice. Such is the message of TULIP.

Considering himself one of the elect, Piper finds great joy in TULIP and expresses no regrets for the predestined fate of those for whom this doctrine could only cause eternal anguish:

> We need to rethink our Reformed doctrine of salvation so that every limb and every branch in the tree is coursing with the sap of Augustinian delight. We need to make plain that *total depravity* is not just badness, but blindness...and *unconditional election* means that the completeness of our joy in Jesus was planned for us before we ever existed [never mind that eternal doom was also planned for others]; and that *limited atonement* is the assurance that indestructible joy in God is infallibly secured for us [the elect for whom alone Christ died] by the blood of the covenant; and *irresistible grace* is the commitment and power of God's love...the *perseverance of the saints* is the almighty work of God to keep us....[13] (Emphasis in original)

What Love, Compassion, and Grace Is THIS?

The elect alone enjoy the "Augustinian delight" of having been chosen to salvation. What delight is there for those who, before they came into existence, were already predestined to eternal torment? Nor can the Calvinist have the slightest sympathy for those whom God has, for His good pleasure, doomed eternally.

In contrast, consider the Bible's repeated assurance that God's love and grace toward all mankind are boundless and eternal. Here are just a few scriptures among many to that effect:

- For the LORD your God is gracious and merciful, and will not turn away his face from you, if ye return unto him. (2 Chronicles 30:9)

- Thou art a God ready to pardon, gracious and merciful, slow to anger, and of great kindness...for thou art a gracious and merciful God. (Nehemiah 9:17,31)

- But thou, O Lord, art a God full of compassion, and gracious, longsuffering, and plenteous in mercy and truth. (Psalm 86:15)

- The LORD is gracious and full of compassion. (Psalms 111:4; 112:4; 145:8, etc.)

- And rend your heart, and not your garments, and turn unto the LORD your God: for he is gracious and merciful.... (Joel 2:13)

- For I knew that thou art a gracious God, and merciful,...of great kindness. (Jonah 4:2)

Like hundreds of others, each of these scriptures is addressed to all of Israel, most of whom rejected God's grace. Never is there any hint that God's merciful compassion extends to less than all. "We love him because he first loved us" (1 John 4:19) declares that our love is in response to God's love. Nowhere does Scripture indicate that we love God, as Piper exults, because we are among a select group whom He predestined to salvation and sovereignly regenerated.

What about those allegedly not chosen to salvation, whom God never intended to save, for whom Christ did not die, and for whom there is no hope? Is it not sadistic to command *them* to love God? Yet this very first of the Ten Commandments, like all of them, is a command to all. How could the non-elect love God when God doesn't love them? Such teaching dishonors God and can only cause resentment toward Him.

Sadly, in reading scores of books by Calvinists, one finds much that extols God's sovereignty but almost nothing of His love. Packer admits, "In Reformation days as since, treatments of God's love in election were often...preempted by wrangles of an abstract sort about God's sovereignty in reprobation."[14] What else has Calvinism to offer!?

As Piper declares, "The doctrine of irresistible grace means that God is sovereign and can overcome all resistance when He wills."[15]

The Christian is to love others with God's love as his strength and example, for "love is of God" (1 John 4:7), "...the love of God is shed abroad in our hearts by the Holy Ghost, which is given unto us" (Romans 5:5), "Ye yourselves are taught of God to love one another" (1 Thessalonians 4:9).

God's love flowing through the believer has a practical effect: "But whoso hath this world's good, and seeth his brother have need, and shutteth up his bowels of compassion from him, how dwelleth the love of God in him?" (1 John 3:17). We are commanded to love our enemies and to do good to all, even to those who hate us (Matthew 5:44; Luke 6:35, etc.).

How odd that God's love dwelling in us would unfailingly meet through us the needs of others—yet God himself sees billions in the direst of need and refuses to help them—indeed, damns those He could save. Surely this is not the God portrayed in the Bible!

A Longsuffering God

Sovereignty in Calvinism, as we have seen, is such that God is behind every emotion and act of every individual, causing each sin and causing each impulse of "love." Supposedly the heart of man is "made willing" in order to love God. But "made willing" is an oxymoron. One can be persuaded or convinced but not *made* willing, because the will must be willing in and of itself.

Again we are compelled to ask, "What love is this?" If Calvin's God can be said to love at all, it is with a love that allegedly can be imposed upon *anyone* and man's response is by that same imposition. But such is not the nature of love.

By contrast, in the Bible God's infinite love, grace, and mercy are demonstrated powerfully in His dealings with Israel. Moreover, the rejection and hatred against Him by disobedient Israel cause God's true love to shine all the brighter. Though himself a Calvinist, D. A. Carson expresses the contradiction of Calvinism clearly:

> The entire prophecy of Hosea is an astonishing portrayal of the love of God. Almighty God is likened to a betrayed and cuckolded husband. But the intensity of God's passion for the covenant nation comes to a climax in Hosea 11. "When Israel was a child," God declares, "I loved him, and out of Egypt I called my son: (11:1)...." But the more God loved Israel, the more they drifted away. God was the one who cared for them...the one who "led them with cords of love and human kindness" (11:4). Yet they... "Sacrificed to Baals and loved idolatry." So God promises judgment. They will return to "Egypt" and Assyria, i.e., to captivity and slavery,

"because they refuse to repent" (11:5). Their cities will be destroyed (11:6).... Thus it sounds as if implacable judgment has been pronounced. But then it is almost as if God cannot endure the thought. In an agony of emotional intensity, God cries,

> "How can I give you up, Ephraim?
> How can I hand you over, Israel?...
> My heart is changed within me;
>   all my compassion is aroused.
> I will not carry out my fierce anger....
>   For I am God, and not man...
>   I will not come in wrath....
> I will settle them in their homes,"
>   declares the LORD.[16]

Yet if Calvinism be true, these pleadings are a sham. The elect don't need them, and the non-elect can't heed them. The totally depraved who are elected to salvation must be regenerated and infused with Irresistible Grace, while the rest of mankind are damned without remedy. Why pretend this love and concern when man has no choice and God can irresistably make anyone do whatever He wants?

Supposedly, to save only a select elect and to damn the rest was necessary to prove God's sovereignty and justice, and will eternally be to His greater glory. Obviously, however, God need not damn anyone in order to prove either His sovereignty or justice. If it is not a threat to God's sovereignty to save the elect, neither would it be for Him to save a million more, 100 million more—or more loving yet, to save all mankind.

Scores of Bible passages leave no doubt that God loves and desires to bless not just an elect who will be redeemed out of Israel, but all of Israel (and therefore all mankind as well), including those who refuse His love and gracious offer of blessing. God's very character is reflected in the commandments He gave to His chosen people. They were to restore even to an enemy his ox or ass that had wandered off (Exodus 23:4). Yet God himself won't give wandering mankind the kindness He commands that man give to beasts? Such teaching doesn't ring true to Scripture or to the conscience God has placed within each person (Romans 2:14–15).

A Foundational Misunderstanding

How does this grievous libel upon God's holy character arise among true Christians? Chiefly through an overemphasis upon the sovereignty of God to the exclusion of all else. It is imagined that if man can make a choice—if even with the wooing and winning of the Holy Spirit he can willingly, from his heart, respond to the love of God in the gospel—God's sovereignty has been nullified. Pink insists that if man could, by an act of his will, believe on and receive Christ, "then the Christian would have ground for boasting and self-glorying over *his* cooperation with the Spirit...."[17] Even Carson, in a book that has so much balanced truth to offer, falls into this error:

> If Christ died for all people with exactly the same intent... then surely it is impossible to avoid the conclusion that the *ultimate* distinguishing mark between those who are saved and those who are not is their own decision, their own will. That is surely ground for boasting.[18]

Only a Calvinist could fail to see the fallacy of this argument. Salvation is "the gift of God" (Romans 6:23). How could a gift be received without the ability to choose? The ability to say no—which is all Calvinism grants to the totally depraved—is meaningless without the accompanying ability to say yes.

Furthermore, how could accepting a gift provide a basis for boasting? If the gift is offered to all freely for the taking, those who receive the gift have no basis whatsoever for giving any credit to themselves. All has been provided in Christ, it is His work, to Him is all the glory, and it is absurd to suggest that the hopeless sinner who has been rescued without merit or effort on his part, but simply by receiving God's grace, could thereby boast of anything.

The Calvinist is so fearful that any response on man's part would challenge God's sovereignty that he invents ever more untenable arguments. Charles Hodge insists that "if efficacious grace is the exercise of almighty power it is irresistible."[19] Following the same reasoning, C. D. Cole writes, "The power of grace is the power of God. This makes it fitting to speak of irresistible grace. Surely we can speak of an irresistible God!"[20]

The flaw in such reasoning is elementary. Omnipotent power has nothing to do with grace or love or bestowing a gift. Indeed, just as God himself cannot force anyone to love Him (a coerced response is the opposite of love), so it would be the very opposite of grace to force any gift or benefit of "grace" upon anyone who did not want to receive it. To be a gift, it must be received willingly. *Power* has nothing to do with God's gracious, loving gift.

Beck, like so many Calvinists, echoes the same unsound argument: "I repeat, the Gospel of Christ *is* the power of God unto salvation! *Nothing* can stop it.... If God's grace can be *successfully* resisted, then *God* can be overcome...."[21] Such arguments are an embarrassment to sound reason. God's power in salvation refers to His ability to pay sin's penalty so that He can be just and yet justify sinners; it does not refer to His forcing salvation upon those who would otherwise reject it. Nowhere in Scripture is there such a concept. Always it is "whosoever *will* may come"—never the imposition of God's grace upon any unwilling person. Here we must agree with Arminius, who said, "Grace is not an omnipotent act of God, which cannot be resisted by the free-will of men."[22] It cannot be, or it would not be grace by very definition.

Yahweh sent His prophets generation after generation to plead for repentance from a people who steadfastly refused the offer of His grace. Why was that grace not "irresistible"? If God's omnipotent power can cause whomever He wills to receive the gift of His grace, then "gift" is no more gift, "grace" is no more grace, and man is not a morally responsible being.

In all of God's pleadings with Israel for her repentance and His promises of blessing if she would do so, there is *never* any suggestion that He could or would impose His grace upon her irresistibly. No Calvinist has ever given a biblical explanation for Irresistible Grace.

As only one of many examples, God cries, "Oh that my people had hearkened unto me...! I should soon have subdued their enemies, [and] have fed them also with the finest of the wheat" (Psalm 81:8–16). Instead, God's judgment fell upon Israel. Was judgment what He intended all along, and were His pleadings insincere? One is driven to such a conclusion by Calvinism—which undermines all of Scripture. Such pleadings with Israel, and with all mankind, are turned into a shameful pretense.

More Contradictions

This elementary but sincere misunderstanding of omnipotence is foundational to Calvinism. Tom Ross argues: "If every man possesses a free will that is powerful enough to resist the will of God in salvation, what would prevent that same man from choosing to resist the will of God in damnation at the great white throne of judgment?"[23] Ross is confused. Those gathered before the great white throne are there because they have repeatedly hardened themselves against God's love and gracious offer of salvation. Now they face His judgment. Grace is *offered* in love; judgment is *imposed* by justice and power.

Can Ross see no difference between salvation offered in God's grace, and judgment imposed by His justice? Can he be serious in suggesting that because the former could be rejected so could the latter? Not all Calvinists agree. Thus Carson writes that "God's unconditioned sovereignty and the responsibility of human beings are mutually compatible."[24]

We do not minimize God's sovereignty—but that must be balanced with His other attributes. Carson declares, "I do not think that what the Bible says about the love of God can long survive at the forefront of our thinking if it is abstracted from the sovereignty of God, the holiness of God, the wrath of God, the providence of God, or the personhood of God—to mention only a few nonnegotiable elements of basic Christianity."[25]

God's absolute sovereignty did not prevent rebellion by Satan and Adam, man's continual disobedience of the Ten Commandments, and his straying like a lost sheep in rejection of God's will. Much less does sovereignty mean that God is behind it all, *causing* every sin—as Calvinism requires. This error gave rise to the belief that grace must be irresistible.

Every conscience bears witness to Carson's un-Calvinistic statement that "The Scriptures do not mock us when they say, 'Like as a father pitieth his children, so the Lord pitieth them that fear him.'"[26] Yet Carson remains a Calvinist while contradicting in many ways what most of his colleagues believe.

Some Calvinists attempt to escape the horrifying consequences of their doctrine by suggesting that predestination unto damnation, and God's invitation to all to believe, are both true even though they contradict each other. Supposedly, we just don't know how to reconcile these apparent conflicts and should not attempt to, for all will be revealed in eternity.

The truth is that Calvinism itself has created this particular "mystery." Although there is much that finite beings cannot understand, we have been given a conscience with a keen sense of right and wrong, and of justice and injustice. God calls us to reason with Him about these things. He goes to great lengths to explain His justice and love, and has given even to unregenerate man the capacity to understand the gospel, and to believe in Christ or to reject Him. Calvinism, as we have repeatedly seen, is repugnant to the God-given conscience.

Irresistible Grace and the Gospel

Most Calvinists attempt to honor Christ's command to "preach the gospel to every creature." Yet it is difficult to uphold the importance of the gospel when the unregenerate are unable to believe it, and the elect are regenerated without it, then sovereignly and supernaturally given faith to believe. Seemingly unaware that he is contradicting the very "Reformed Theology" of which he is a major defender, Sproul earnestly exhorts readers, "If we believe in the power of the gospel to effect our salvation, we must believe in the power of the Gospel preached to bring in His elect."[27] But Calvinism's elect have been predestined from a past eternity, and it is God's sovereign act of regeneration, *not the gospel,* which alone can "bring in His elect."

Given **TULIP**, how can the gospel effect the salvation of anyone? The unregenerate, elect or non-elect, cannot respond to or believe it. Nor would it benefit the non-elect to understand, because they have been predestined to eternal damnation from the beginning.

The elect are regenerated without the gospel and only then can they believe it. But once regenerated, they have already been saved unless one can be sovereignly regenerated (i.e., born again by the Spirit) and still not be saved. Having been regenerated without the gospel, subsequently hearing and believing it cannot save them, since they have already been saved in their regeneration.

Sproul is being faithful to God's Word, which clearly teaches that the gospel "is the power of God unto salvation to every one that believeth" it (Romans 1:16). In being true to the Bible, however, he must ignore Calvinism's teaching that one cannot believe the gospel until one has been regenerated. So he talks as though the gospel, as the Bible says, must be believed for salvation—but he cannot truly believe this, or he would have to abandon Calvinism.

Sproul spends an entire book rightly rebuking the signers of "Evangelicals and Catholics Together: The Christian Mission in the Third Millennium." He argues correctly that

"Justification by faith alone is essential to the gospel. The gospel is essential to Christianity and to salvation."[28] He ends the book with this un-Calvinistic quote from John Calvin: "Let it therefore remain settled...that we are justified by faith alone."[29]

But Sproul believes there is no faith until regeneration, so the new birth into God's family as a child of God leaves one still unjustified! Furthermore, since faith in Christ through the gospel is essential to salvation, we have the elect born again as children of God before they are saved.

When it deals with the gospel, Calvinism becomes very confusing. How can the gospel preached "bring in His elect" as Sproul declares? Even the elect can't believe it until they have been regenerated—and Calvinism is firm that regeneration is the way for God to "bring in His elect." Was it not the sovereign act of regeneration that brought the elect into the fold? Then the gospel was not involved, and Sproul is offering false motivation for preaching it.

The Calvinist apparently has two compartments in his mind: in one, he holds to Calvinism's dogmas faithfully, and in the other, he holds to the teaching of Scripture. It can't be easy or comfortable for the conscience. The fact that faith in Christ through the gospel precedes the new birth/salvation (in contradiction to the doctrine of regeneration before faith) is undeniably taught in scores of passages such as the following:

- The devil...taketh away the word out of their hearts, lest they should believe and be saved. (Luke 8:12)

- Believe on the Lord Jesus Christ, and thou shalt be saved.... (Acts 16:31)

- That if thou shalt...believe in thine heart...thou shalt be saved. (Romans 10:9)

- In whom [Christ] also ye trusted, *after* that ye heard the word of truth, the *gospel* of your *salvation*: in whom also *after that ye believed*, ye were sealed with that holy Spirit of promise....(Ephesians 1:13; emphasis added)

A Classic Oxymoron

On its very face, the phrase "Irresistible Grace" presents another irreconcilable contradiction. As far as grace is concerned, there are two possible meanings for the word "irresistible": irresistible in its appeal to all mankind; or irresistible in its imposition upon the elect alone. The former is, of course, vigorously denied by Calvinism. That system is founded upon the belief that grace and the gospel have no appeal at all to the totally depraved, spiritually dead sons and daughters of Adam. Nor does grace have any appeal even to the elect until they have been sovereignly regenerated.

Only one possibility remains: that grace is irresistibly imposed upon a chosen elect—and this is the teaching of Calvinism. But to impose anything upon anyone is the very antithesis of grace. Forcing even a most valuable and desirable gift upon someone who does not wish to receive it would be ungracious in the extreme. Thus the phrase "Irresistible Grace" is another oxymoron. Yet this is an integral element without which the other four points of TULIP collapse.

Moreover, this fourth point of TULIP, like the first three, confronts us with one more phrase unknown to Scripture—

so how can it possibly be biblical? The word "irresistible" does not appear in the Bible. The wonderful grace of God, however, is one of the most precious truths presented in His Word. The word "grace" occurs 170 times in 159 verses. And *never* in *any* mention of it is there a suggestion that grace is irresistibly imposed. Always the inference is that God's grace is given freely and willingly received.

Consider a few examples:

- But Noah found grace in the eyes of the LORD. (Genesis 6:8)

- The LORD will give grace and glory.... (Psalm 84:11)

- By whom we have received grace and apostleship.... (Romans 1:5)

- Having then gifts differing according to the grace that is given to us.... (Romans 12:6)

- I thank my God...for the grace of God which is given you by Jesus Christ.... (1 Corinthians 1:4)

- Unto me, who am less than the least of all saints, is this grace given.... (Ephesians 3:8)

- But unto every one of us is given grace according to the measure of the gift of Christ. (Ephesians 4:7)

- Likewise, ye husbands...giving honour unto the wife...as being heirs together of the grace of life.... (1 Peter 3:7)

What about other scriptures, such as "And I will pour upon the house of David, and upon the inhabitants of Jerusalem, the spirit of grace and supplications..." (Zechariah 12:10); "And with great power gave the apostles witness...and great grace was upon them" (Acts 4:33); "And God is able to make all grace abound toward you..." (2 Corinthians 9:8), etc.? Although the indication seems stronger that God is sovereignly grant-ing grace, there is no indication that God's grace is irresistibly imposed upon anyone. Each must, of his own will, choose to receive it.

The "Two Conflicting Wills" Theory Revisited

Many Calvinists, in upholding that system, make astonishing statements such as the following: "Because God's will is always done, the will of every creature must conform to the sovereign will of God."[30] Logically, then, *every thought, word, and deed* of mankind (including the most heinous wickedness) has been willed by God. Vance comments, "That fornication and unthankfulness are actually part of God's 'secret will' should come as no surprise in light of...the Calvinistic concept of God's all-encompassing decree."[31] But does not everyone's God-given conscience shrink in horror from this doctrine that all evil is according to God's will? Pink even rejects the distinction sometimes made between God's "perfect will" and His "permissive will," because "God only permits that which is according to His will."[32] He thus contradicts MacArthur's view of 1 Timothy 2:4 that God has two conflicting wills—a view with which Sproul, Piper, and other leading Calvinists are in full agreement.

Calvinists struggle to reconcile a sovereignty that causes every sinful thought, word, and deed and damns billions, with the repeated biblical assurances of God's goodness, compassion, and love for all. Much like MacArthur, John Piper proposes an unbiblical and irrational solution—the idea that God has *two wills* that contradict one another yet are not in conflict:

> Therefore I affirm with John 3:16 and 1 Timothy 2:4 that God loves the world with a deep compassion that desires the salvation of all men. Yet I also affirm that God has chosen from before the foundation of the world whom he will save from sin. Since not all people are saved we must choose whether we believe (with the Arminians) that God's will to save all people is restrained by his commitment to human self-determination or whether we believe (with the Calvinists) that God's will to save all people is restrained by his commitment to the glorification of his sovereign grace (Ephesians 1:6, 12, 14; Romans 9:22–23).... This book aims to show that the sovereignty of God's grace in salvation is taught in Scripture. My contribution has simply been to show that God's will for all people to be saved is not at odds with the sovereignty of God's grace in election. That is, my answer to the question about what restrains God's will to save all people is his supreme commitment to uphold and display the full range of his glory through the sovereign demonstration of his wrath and mercy for the enjoyment of his elect and believing people from every tribe and tongue and nation.[33]

Once again, we have an unblushing contradiction from Piper. In His great love and compassion, God "desires the salvation of all men." Yet to "display the full range of his glory" he doesn't save them all—and this in spite of the insistence that He could save all if he so desired. Let us get this straight: Piper's God desires the salvation of all men; in His sovereign imposition of irresistible grace, he *could* save all but doesn't in order to demonstrate his wrath.

Here we have the clearest contradiction possible. How can the Calvinist escape? Ah, Piper has found an ingenious way to affirm that God loves and really desires to save even those whom He has predestined to damnation from eternity past: God has *two wills* which, though they contradict each other, are really in secret agreement. Are we being led into madness where words have lost their meaning?

We are asked to believe that it is no contradiction for God to contradict himself if it furthers the "sovereign demonstration of his wrath and mercy"! Reason fails Piper once again. Damning billions would certainly demonstrate God's wrath— but how would that glorify Him in his mercy? And even if that somehow were the case, there is no way to reconcile reprobation with the clear expressions of God's love and desire for the salvation of all—expressions which Piper uncalvinistically claims to accept at face value.

Piper has yet another problem. God does not contradict Himself. Therefore, Piper must reconcile what he calls "two wills" of God to show that they are in agreement, even though they directly disagree with and invalidate each other. And this he fails to do, because it is impossible. A contradiction is a contradiction, and there is no honest way that two contradictory propositions can be massaged into agreement.

Piper is following Calvin, who fell into the same misconception. He said, "This is His wondrous love towards the human race, that He desires all men to be saved, and is prepared to bring even the perishing to safety.... God is prepared to receive all men into repentance, so that none may perish."[34] Could this be the same John Calvin who declared so often and so clearly that, from a past eternity, God had predestined billions to damnation? Is Calvin's God a schizophrenic?

Very much like Piper's "two wills," Calvin fell back upon a "secret will": "No mention is made here of the secret decree of God by which the wicked are doomed to their own ruin."[35] Sproul attempts to play the same broken string. Bryson responds reasonably and succinctly:

> Thus, Calvinists are in the rather awkward position of claiming to make a valid offer of salvation (to the unelect)...while denying [that] the only provision (i.e., Christ's death) of salvation is for the unelect...[and saying] that the unelect cannot possibly believe [the gospel].... To add insult to injury, they are claiming this is just the way God (from all eternity) wanted it to be.[36]

Calvinists claim that man's will and actions cannot be in conflict with God's will, for that would make man greater than God. That unbiblical position concerning God's sovereignty drives them to propose that the two wills in conflict are not God's will and man's will, but two wills of God's design. In other words, they claim that the battle is not between God and man, as the Bible says, but rather God against himself, as Calvinism insists. God is being misrepresented.

1. Loraine Boettner, *The Reformed Doctrine of Predestination* (Phillipsburg, NJ: Presbyterian and Reformed Publishing Co., 1932), 365.

2. Benjamin B. Warfield, *Calvin and Augustine*, ed. Samuel G. Craig (Phillipsburg, NJ: Presbyterian and Reformed Publishing Co., 1956), 321.

3. Kenneth H. Good, *Are Baptists Calvinists?* (Rochester, NY: Backus Book Publishers, 1988), 49.

4. R. C. Sproul, *The Holiness of God* (Carol Stream, IL: Tyndale House Publishers, Inc., 1993 ed.), 273.

5. William G. T. Shedd, *A History of Christian Doctrine* (New York: Charles Scribner and Co., 3rd ed. 1865), 70.

6. Augustine, *On the Spirit and the Letter.* In Laurence M. Vance, *The Other Side of Calvinism* (Pensacola, FL: Vance Publications, rev. ed. 1999), 57.

7. Augustine, *On the Predestination of the Saints*, op. cit., 7,8,16.

8. Dave Breese, "The Five Points of Calvinism" (self-published paper, n. d.), 3.

9. John Piper and Pastoral Staff, "TULIP: What We Believe about the Five Points of Calvinism: Position Paper of the Pastoral Staff" (Minneapolis, MN: Desiring God Ministries, 1997), 12.

10. Piper and Staff, "TULIP," 9.

11. Ibid.

12. Charles Hodge, *Systematic Theology* (Grand Rapids, MI: Wm B. Eerdmans Publishing Co., 1986), 2:643.

13. John Piper, *The Legacy of Sovereign Joy: God's Triumphant Grace in the Lives of Augustine, Luther, and Calvin* (Wheaton, IL: Crossway Books, 2000), 73.

14. J. I. Packer, "The Love of God: Universal and Particular," in *Still Sovereign,* ed. Thomas R. Schreiner and Bruce A. Ware (Grand Rapids, MI: Baker Books, 2000) 281.

15. Piper and Staff, "TULIP," 9.

16. D. A. Carson, *The Difficult Doctrine of the Love of God* (Wheaton, IL: Crossway Books, 2000), 46–47.

17. Arthur W. Pink, *The Sovereignty of God* (Grand Rapids, MI: Baker Book House, 2nd prtg. 1986), 128.

18. Carson, *Difficult*, 78–79.

19. Hodge, *Systematic*, II:687.

20. C. D. Cole, *Definitions of Doctrines* (Swengle, PA: Bible Truth Depot, n. d.), 84.

21. Frank B. Beck, *The Five Points of Calvinism* (Lithgow, Australia: Covenanter Press, 2nd Australian ed. 1986), 40.

22. Jacobus Arminius, *The Works of James Arminius*, trans. James and William Nichols (Grand Rapids, MI: Baker Book House, 1986), I:525.

23. Tom Ross, *Abandoned Truth: The Doctrines of Grace* (Providence Baptist Church, 1991), 56.

24. Carson, *Difficult*, 52.

25. Ibid., 11.

26. Ibid., 29.

27. R. C. Sproul, Jr., "The Authentic Message," *Tabletalk*, Ligonier Ministries, Inc., June 2001, 7.

28. R. C. Sproul, *Faith Alone: The Evangelical Doctrine of Justification* (Grand Rapids, MI: Baker Books, 1995), 19, and throughout the book.

29. Ibid., 192; citing Calvin, *The Epistles of Paul the Apostle* (a comment on Galatians 2:16), 39.

30. Steven R. Houck, *The Bondage of the Will* (Lansing, IL: Peace Protestant Reformed Church, n. d.), 3.

31. Laurence M. Vance, *The Other Side of Calvinism* (Pensacola, FL: Vance Publications, rev. ed. 1999), 481.

32. Pink, *Sovereignty*, 243.

33. John Piper, "Are There Two Wills In God?" In *Still Sovereign*, ed. Thomas R. Schreiner and Bruce A. Ware (Grand Rapids, MI: Baker Books, 2000), 130–31.

34. John Calvin, *Calvin's New Testament Commentaries* (Grand Rapids, MI: Wm B. Eerdmans Publishing Co., 1994), 12, 364.

35. Ibid.

36. George L. Bryson, *The Five Points of Calvinism: Weighed and Found Wanting* (Costa Mesa, CA: The Word For Today, 1996), 56.

"P" is for "Perseverance of the Saints"

BEFORE BEGINNING what turned into an urgent and in-depth study of Calvinism, I had thought that I was at least a one-point Calvinist. Surely my belief in eternal security—the assurance of living eternally in God's presence through being redeemed by Christ and kept secure in Him—must be the same as Calvinism's Perseverance of the Saints. That turned out, however, not to be the case, and I was surprised to discover why.

Biblical assurance of salvation does not depend upon one's performance, but upon the gospel truth that Christ died for the sins of the world, and upon His promise that whosoever believes in Him receives the free and unconditional gift of eternal life.

In contrast, the Calvinist's assurance is in God's having pre-destined him to eternal life as one of the elect. Coppes insists that "God's answer to doubt...the only proper fount of assurance of salvation...of getting to heaven (glorification) is the doctrine of predestination."[1] That view has serious problems, as we shall see. How does the Calvinist know he is one of the elect who have been predestined? His performance plays a large part in helping him to know whether or not he is among that select group.

In contrast, my faith, hope, trust, and confidence is in my Savior the Lord Jesus Christ, who paid on the Cross the full penalty for my sins. Therefore, according to His promise, which I have believed, my sins are forgiven. I have been born again into God's family as His dear child. Heaven is my eternal home. My hope is in Christ alone.

Christ calls, "Come unto me, all ye that labour and are heavy laden, and I will give you rest" (Matthew 11:28). Laden with sin, I came to Him and, as He promised, found eternal rest in Him alone. Christ guarantees, "him that cometh to me I will in no wise cast out" (John 6:37). I came to Him by faith in His Word and He will never cast me out—i.e., I can never be lost. My assurance is in His promise and keeping power, not in my efforts or performance. He said, "I give unto them [my sheep] eternal life; and they shall never perish" (John 10:28). It would be strange "eternal life" indeed if it were mine today by His gracious gift and taken away by His judgment tomorrow.

Yet many professing Christians (including many Five-Point Calvinists who believe in Perseverance of the Saints) are troubled with doubts concerning their salvation. Doubts even assail leading Calvinists.

Zane C. Hodges points out that "The result of this theology is disastrous. Since, according to Puritan belief, the genuineness of a man's faith can only be determined by the life that follows it, assurance of salvation becomes impossible at the moment of conversion."[2] And, one might add, at any time thereafter as well, if one's life ever fails to meet the biblical standard.

Piper and his staff write, "[W]e must also own up to the fact that our final salvation is made contingent upon the subsequent obedience which comes from faith."[3] Small comfort or assurance in *my* ability to obey! Indeed, the fifth point *is* called perseverance *of the saints*, putting the burden on me. No wonder, then, as R. T. Kendall has commented, that "nearly all of the Puritan 'divines' went through great doubt and despair on their deathbeds as they realized their lives did not give perfect evidence that they were elect."[4]

Arminius, on the other hand, contrary to the false label attached to him by his enemies, had perfect assurance. He confidently declared that the believer can "depart out of this life...to appear before the throne of grace, without any anxious fear...."[5]

An Endemic Uncertainty of Salvation

Oddly, the reason for such uncertainty among Calvinists is found where one would expect assurance—in the "P" of TULIP: Perseverance of the *Saints*. Clearly, the emphasis is upon the *believer's* faithfulness in persevering—not upon God's keeping power.

Strangely enough, certainty of salvation and confidence of one's eternal destiny are not to be found in the fifth point of Calvinism where one would expect it. Nor can they be found in the other four points. Although many Calvinists would deny it, uncertainty as to one's ultimate salvation is, in fact, built into the very fabric of Calvinism itself.

Congdon writes, *"Absolute assurance of salvation is impossible in Classical Calvinism...*[emphasis his]. Understand why: Since works are an *inevitable* outcome of 'true' salvation, one can only know he or she is saved by the presence of good works. But since no one is perfect...any assurance is at best imperfect as well. Therefore, you may *think* you believed in Jesus Christ, may *think* you had saving faith, but be sadly mistaken...and because unsaved, be totally blind to the fact you are unsaved...! R. C. Sproul...in an article entitled 'Assurance of Salvation,' writes: 'There are people in this world who are not saved, but who are convinced that they are....'

"When our assurance of salvation is based *at all* on our works, we can never have absolute assurance...! But does Scripture discourage giving objective assurance of salvation? Hardly! On the contrary, the Lord Jesus (John 5:24), Paul (Romans 8:38–39), and John (1 John 5:11–13) have no qualms about offering absolute, objective assurance of salvation. Furthermore, works are *never* included as a requirement for assurance."[6]

Bob Wilkin of Grace Evangelical Society reports what he heard at Sproul's Ligonier National Conference (with about 5,000 present), June 15–17, 2000 in Orlando, Florida:

> John Piper...described himself as "a seven point Calvinist"...[and said] that no Christian can be sure he is a true believer; hence there is an ongoing need to be dedicated to the Lord and deny ourselves so that we might make it. [We must endure to the end in faith if we are to be saved.[7]]
>
> This struck me as odd, since there was so much emphasis on the sovereignty of God in this conference. Yet when it comes right down to it, within a Reformed

perspective God uses fear of hell to motivate Christians to live for Him.

My heart is heavy as I write this from Orlando. I feel such a burden for the people here. Why? Because their theology makes assurance impossible. It [lack of assurance] permeated the whole conference.[8]

What a commentary, that lack of assurance of salvation permeated the Ligonier National Conference featuring major Calvinist speakers! Why should that be? Because the Calvinist cannot rely upon Christ's promise of eternal life in the gospel (since that promise is for the elect alone), his security lies in being one of the elect—but how can he be certain that he is? Piper writes, "We believe in eternal security...the eternal security of the elect."[9] And there one confronts a serious problem: How can any Calvinist be certain that he is among that select company predestined for heaven? He can't. There is not a verse in the Bible telling anyone how to be certain that he is among the elect.

Though Christ commanded that the gospel be preached to every person living in the entire world, the Calvinist says it is effective for only the elect. Others can *imagine* they believe the gospel, but not having been sovereignly regenerated, their faith is not from God and will not save. As Sproul and his fellow editors declare, "The fruit of regeneration is faith. Regeneration precedes faith."[10]

Indeed, the gospel offers false hope to the non-elect and, in fact, condemns them. Thus, believing the gospel is of no value unless one has first been sovereignly regenerated by God without faith, having been predestined to salvation. Yet predestination was determined by God in eternity past and, as Packer writes, "decreed by his counsel secret to us"[11]—so how can that doctrine give assurance to anyone today? Who can know that he is among the secretly predestined elect?

No wonder, then, that many Calvinists are plagued by doubts concerning their salvation. When facing such doubts, VanOverloop gives the cheering advice to "wait prayerfully for a season of richer grace."[12] Otis, on the other hand, suggests that "One of the proofs that we are genuinely saved is that our faith will persevere to the end of our lives."[13] But what if doubts come, such as confronted "nearly all of the Puritan 'divines'"?

Disagreement on a Vital Point

Admittedly, there is no general agreement on this point. Many Calvinists do affirm that believing the gospel brings assurance. In a Calvinist symposium, the essay on assurance by D. A. Carson, which attempts to give a balanced biblical view, does not offer any typical Calvinist arguments for Perseverance of the Saints at all and comes to no definitive conclusion.[14] As we have seen, Calvin taught that being born into a Calvinist family automatically made the child one of the elect, as did infant baptism, so long as one believed in its efficacy. Thus, while believing the gospel is no sure way to be saved, believing in one's infant baptism is.

Sproul declares, "Infants can be born again, although the faith they exercise cannot be as visible as that of adults."[15] Infants have *faith* in Christ—it is just less visible? Does Sproul or any other Calvinist really believe that?

For the Calvinist, moreover, seeking assurance that one's faith is genuine raises further difficulties, because faith is a gift from God and has nothing to do with man's volition. But how can one know whether one's faith is a gift from God, or originates in his own mind and will?

Dillow quotes Dabney that each one must examine his faith, because it is possible to have a false faith. This only raises further questions. Would God give false faith? Calvin said He would and does. So if God gives true faith to some and false faith to others, how could one know whether the faith he thinks he has is genuine? Who could stand up to a delusion from God? And how would infants examine their "faith"?

Yet Boettner carries on at length about faith being the assurance that one is among the elect, and he argues that since faith "is not given to any but the elect only, the person who knows that he has this faith can be assured that he is among the elect."[16] But what about the false faith and assurance that Calvin says God gives to the non-elect, the better to damn them? The *Geneva Study Bible* makes no mention of that problem and even suggests that John wrote his first epistle "to assure those who have believed that they actually possess the priceless gift [of eternal life]."[17] How can leading Calvinists be so ignorant of what John Calvin taught?

Attempting to fortify his argument from a different angle, Boettner writes, "Every person who loves God and has a true desire for salvation in Christ is among the elect, for the non-elect never have this love or this desire."[18] By that standard, however, the Christians in the church at Ephesus would have doubted their salvation because they no longer had that fervent love (Revelation 2:4–5)—yet there is no suggestion that they were not true Christians.

The Puritans struggled with this very question. Dillow accuses Dabney of vainly trying to defend an "issue which dominated three hundred years of English Puritan debate"[19]— considerable dissension indeed, and on a very key point. Arminius, however, declared, "[M]y opinion is, that it is possible for him who believes in Jesus Christ to be certain...that he is a son of God, and stands in the grace of Jesus Christ."[20]

Dillow, though a staunch Calvinist, disagrees that faith must be examined. He argues, "The Bible never raises this issue.... Does a man struggle to know if he loves his child...? We know we have believed aright if we have believed according to biblical truth.... The issue is not a rational examination of our faith...[but] a rational examination of the object of faith, Jesus Christ, and the gospel offer."[21] He goes on to accuse fellow Calvinists of being taken up with preserving a dogma:

> Finally, the Bible explicitly and implicitly affirms that assurance is part of saving faith.... "Faith is the assurance of things hoped for" (Hebrews 11:1). But in addition, the scores of passages which tell us that "whosoever believes has eternal life" surely imply that a person who has believed has eternal life.... Belief and assurance are so obviously inseparable that only the interest of preserving the Experimental Predestinarian doctrine of perseverance can justify their division.[22]

Uncomfortable with Jesus?

Following Calvin's teaching, however, like the Jehovah's Witnesses and Mormons, many Calvinists believe that the only way to make one's "calling and election sure" (2 Peter 1:10) is not through faith but through good works. Oddly, although the first four points of Calvinism insist that man can do nothing, the fifth depends, in the view of many, upon human effort. Boettner quotes Warfield: "It is idle to seek assurance of election outside of holiness of life."[23] Likewise, Charles Hodge declares, "The only evidence of our election...[and] perseverance, is a patient continuance in well-doing."[24]

But finding assurance in one's works always leaves questions unanswered in view of the undeniable fact, which we have commented upon earlier, that the apparent good works of the unsaved sometimes put professed Christians to shame. Furthermore, one's performance could be excellent most of one's life, but if failure comes at some point, one has lost performance-based assurance. R. C. Sproul expressed that very concern for his own salvation:

> A while back I had one of those moments of acute self-awareness...and suddenly the question hit me: "R. C., what if you are not one of the redeemed? What if your destiny is not heaven after all, but hell?" Let me tell you that I was flooded in my body with a chill that went from my head to the bottom of my spine. I was terrified.
>
> I tried to grab hold of myself. I thought, "Well, it's a good sign that I'm worried about this. Only true Christians really care about salvation." But then I began to take stock of my life, and I looked at my

performance. My sins came pouring into my mind, and
the more I looked at myself, the worse I felt. I thought,
"Maybe it's really true. Maybe I'm not saved after all."

I went to my room and began to read the Bible.
On my knees I said, "Well, here I am. I can't point
to my obedience. There's nothing I can offer.... I knew
that some people only flee to the Cross to escape hell....
I could not be sure about my own heart and motivation. Then I remembered John 6:68.... Peter was also
uncomfortable, but he realized that being uncomfortable with Jesus was better than any other option![25]

Uncomfortable with Jesus?! Where is the comfort and
assurance in that? Couldn't a Muslim obtain similar assurance through being *uncomfortable* with Muhammad and the
Qur'an, or a Mormon through being uncomfortable with
Joseph Smith? Why is it better to be uncomfortable with Jesus
than with Buddha? Where does the Bible suggest, much less
commend, being *uncomfortable* with Jesus? Nor is that taught
in this passage. This idea seems all the more pitiful, coming
from a Christian leader and theologian as his assurance that he
is one of the elect!

There is no escaping the necessity of evidence, and solid
faith based upon it, which the Bible and the Holy Spirit provide
in abundance to the believer. Peter could not understand what
Christ meant about eating His body and drinking His blood.
But that did not change the fact that he knew that Jesus was the
Messiah. The important statement from Peter was "Thou hast
the words of eternal life. And we believe and are sure that thou
art that Christ, the Son of the living God" (John 6:68–69).

Such faith, however, is not sufficient to give the Calvinist assurance. It would still leave him uncomfortable because the non-elect often think they believe in Christ. According to Calvin, God even helps them with this delusion. Where is that in the Bible?

We have every reason to be very comfortable with Jesus—and this is one of the great blessings and part of the joy of our salvation. We have absolute proof that the Bible is God's Word, that Jesus is the Christ, that the gospel is true, and we have the witness of the Holy Spirit within. The Bible gives absolute assurance: "These things have I written unto you that believe in the name of the Son of God; that ye may know that ye have eternal life..." (1 John 5:13). That assurance, according to this scripture and many others, is for all those who simply believe in Christ. There is no other basis for assurance of sins forgiven and eternal life.

Why doesn't Sproul rely upon such promises? Because, for a Calvinist, the question is not whether one has believed the gospel but whether one, from eternity past, was predestined by God to be among the elect—and that is an elusive question, as many a Calvinist has discovered to his dismay.

1. Leonard J. Coppes, *Are Five Points Enough? The Ten Points of Calvinism* (Denver, CO: self-published, 1980), 25, 27.

2. Zane C. Hodges, author's preface to *The Gospel Under Siege* (Dallas, TX: Kerugma, Inc., 2nd ed. 1992), vi.

3. John Piper and Pastoral Staff, "TULIP: What We Believe about the Five Points of Calvinism: Position Paper of the Pastoral Staff" (Minneapolis, MN: Desiring God Ministries, 1997) 25.

4. R. T. Kendall, *Calvin and English Calvinism to 1649* (Oxford: Oxford University Press, 1979), 2; cited without page number by Bob Wilkin, "Ligonier National Conference" (*The Grace Report*, July 2000).

5. Jacobus Arminius, *The Works of James Arminius*, trans. James and William Nichols (Grand Rapids,MI: Baker Book House, 1986), 1:667; cited in Laurence M. Vance, *The Other Side of Calvinism* (Pensacola, FL: Vance Publications, rev. ed. 1999), 591.

6. Philip F. Congdon, "Soteriological Implications of Five-point Calvinism," *Journal of the Grace Evangelical Society*, Autumn 1995, 8:15, 55–68.

7. Piper and Staff, TULIP, 23.

8. Wilkin, "Ligonier," 1–2.

9. Piper and Staff, TULIP, 24.

10. *New Geneva Study Bible*, "Regeneration: The New Birth" (Nashville, TN: Thomas Nelson Publishers, 1995), 1664.

11. J. I. Packer, "The Love of God: Universal and Particular." In *Still Sovereign: Contemporary Perspectives on Election, Foreknowledge and Grace*, ed. Thomas R. Schreiner and Bruce A. Ware (Grand Rapids, MI: Baker Books, 2000), 281.

12. Ronald VanOverloop, "Calvinism and Missions: Pt. 2, Unconditional Election" (Grandville, MI: Standard Bearer, January 15, 1993), 185; cited in Vance, *Other Side*, 403.

13. John M. Otis, *Who is the Genuine Christian?* (n. p., n. d.), 39; cited in Vance, *Other Side*, 595.

14. D. A. Carson, "Reflections on Assurance." In Schreiner and Ware, *Still*, 247–48.

15. *New Geneva Study Bible*, 1664.

16. Loraine Boettner, *The Reformed Doctrine of Predestination* (Phillipsburg, NJ: Presbyterian and Reformed Publishing Co., 1932), 308.

17. *New Geneva Study Bible* (marginal note commenting upon 1 John 5:13), 1993.

18. Boettner, *Reformed*, 309.

19. Joseph C. Dillow, *The Reign of the Servant Kings: A Study of Eternal Security and the Final Significance of Man* (Haysville, NC: Schoettle Publishing Co., 2nd ed. 1993), 192–93.

20. Arminius, *Works*, 1:667.

21. Dillow, *Reign*, 193.

22. Ibid., 291.

23. Boettner, *Reformed*, 309.

24. Charles Hodge, *A Commentary on Romans* (Carlisle, PA: The Banner of Truth Trust, 1972), 292.

25. R. C. Sproul, "Assurance of Salvation," *Tabletalk*, Ligonier Ministries, Inc., November 1989, 20.

chapter

Serious Errors, Surprising Tolerance

JOHN CALVIN BELIEVED and practiced a number of things that many of those who call themselves Calvinists today would consider seriously wrong, if not heresy. For example (as we have seen), he dogmatically affirmed the efficacy of infant baptism to effect forgiveness of sins and entrance into the Kingdom. And in spite of his quarrel with Rome, he taught that being baptized by a Roman Catholic priest (done to Calvin as an infant) was efficacious for eternity. The priest could even be a rank unbeliever.

Had he not maintained this Roman Catholic false doctrine, Calvin would have had to submit to rebaptism, which was repugnant to him. He derided the Anabaptists for opposing infant baptism. Their valid, biblical reason—that an infant has not believed in Christ—was scorned by Calvin, and his wrath and that of the other Reformers came upon the Anabaptists. These true evangelicals were persecuted and martyred by both Catholics and Protestants for being baptized by immersion after they were saved by grace alone through faith alone in Christ alone.

Rejection of infant baptism was one of the two charges for which Servetus (prosecuted by Calvin the lawyer) was burned at the stake. Calvin wrote, "One should not be content with simply killing such people, but should burn them cruelly."[1] [See the author's books, *What Love Is This?* or *Calvin's Tyrannical Kingdom* for more details and examples.]

Calvin promotes the error of baptismal regeneration, of salvation by "some secret method...of regenerating" without "the hearing of faith [of the gospel]," that children of the elect are automatically children of God, and of equating circumcision with baptism: "The promise...is one in both [circumcision and baptism]...forgiveness of sins, and eternal life...i.e., regeneration.... Hence we may conclude, that... baptism has been substituted for circumcision, and performs the same office."[2]

Infant Baptism and Circumcision

Nothing more than this section of his *Institutes* is needed to disqualify Calvin as a sound teacher of Scripture and to call into question his entire concept of salvation. His sacramentalism mimics Roman Catholicism:

> We have...a spiritual promise given to the fathers in circumcision, similar to that which is given to us in

baptism...the forgiveness of sins and the mortification of the flesh...baptism representing to us the very thing which circumcision signified to the Jews....

We confess, indeed, that the word of the Lord is the only seed of spiritual regeneration; but we deny... that, therefore, the power of God cannot regenerate infants.... But *faith*, they say, *cometh by hearing*, the use of which infants have not yet obtained....

Let God, then, be demanded why he ordered circumcision to be performed on the bodies of infants... by baptism we are ingrafted into the body of Christ (1 Cor xii.13) [Therefore] infants...are to be baptised....

See the violent onset which they make...on the bulwarks of our faith.... For...children...[of] Christians, as they are immediately on their birth received by God as heirs of the covenant, are also to be admitted to baptism.[3]

This same baptismal regeneration, contempt for believers' baptism, and blindness concerning the difference between circumcision and baptism remains among many Calvinists today. Under the heading, "Infant Baptism," in his Geneva Study Bible, R. C. Sproul echoes Calvin:

Historic Reformed [Calvinist] theology contests the view that only adult, believer's baptism is true baptism, and it rejects the exclusion of believers' children from the visible community of faith.... Rather, the scriptural case for baptizing believers' infants rests on the parallel between Old Testament circumcision and New Testament baptism as signs and seals of the covenant of grace.[4]

On the contrary, baptism belongs to the new covenant and is only upon confession of faith in Christ (Acts 8:37); circumcision was under the old covenant and without faith—and neither one saves the soul. Moreover, not only did circumcision *not* effect regeneration, forgiveness of sins, or salvation, it couldn't even be a symbol thereof, as T. A. McMahon reminds us, being only for males.[5] How could women be saved? And it was for *all* male descendants of Abraham. Even Ishmael, a rank unbeliever, was circumcised—as were millions of Jews.

If, as Calvin taught, circumcision effects "forgiveness of sins, and eternal life...i.e., regeneration,"[6] how could Jews who were circumcised be lost; and why did Paul cry out to God "for Israel...that they might be saved" (Romans 10:1)? Why was he so concerned for the salvation of circumcised Jews that he said, "I could wish that myself were accursed from Christ for my brethren, my kinsmen according to the flesh: who are Israelites..." (Romans 9:1-4)? Clearly, circumcision did not provide "forgiveness of sins and eternal life"—nor does baptism!

Was Calvin Really the Great Exegete?

Calvin's arguments reflect a bias in favor of the sacramentalism he learned as a Roman Catholic from Augustine, which he elaborated upon and thereafter was compelled to defend. His logic often betrays a spiritual immaturity. Incredibly, Calvin argued:

> Such in the present day are our Catabaptists, who deny
> that we are duly baptised, because we were baptised

in the Papacy by wicked men and idolaters.... Against these absurdities we shall be sufficiently fortified if we reflect that by baptism we were initiated...into the name of the Father, and the Son, and the Holy Spirit; and, therefore, that baptism is not of man, but of God, by whomsoever it may have been administered [if clergy].

Be it that those who baptised us were most ignorant of God and all piety, or were despisers, still they did not baptise us into...their ignorance or sacrilege, but into the faith of Jesus Christ, because the name they invoked was not their own but God's.... But if baptism was of God, it certainly included in it the promise of forgiveness of sin, mortification of the flesh, quickening of the Spirit, and communion with Christ.[7]

In Calvinism, the physical act of baptism has spiritual power and imparts regeneration. To be baptized by Roman Catholic priests who were not even Christians, but promoted a false gospel, was acceptable to Calvin because they used the name of God when they administered it! Even to be baptized by *despisers* of Christ and God would bring the "promise of forgiveness of sin..." so long as they were "part of the ministerial office."

Incredibly, though a major figure in the Protestant Reformation, Calvin honored Rome's corrupt and unsaved priests as God's ministers! Yet he condemned and persecuted those who came out of that Antichrist system through faith in Christ for being subsequently baptized as believers according to God's holy Word.

Calvin taught that only the clergy, whether Roman Catholic or Protestant, could baptize or administer the Lord's Supper:

> It...is improper for private individuals to take upon themselves the administration of baptism; for it, as well as the dispensation of the Supper, is part of the ministerial office. For Christ did not give command to any man or woman whatever to baptise, but to those whom he had appointed apostles.[8]

Thus, Calvin also accepted Rome's claim that her bishops were the successors of the twelve Apostles, and from them her priests received divine authority. And he was a leader of the Reformation? Contrary to what Calvin taught about an exclusive "ministerial office," our Lord Jesus Christ clearly commanded the original disciples to make disciples and to teach every disciple they won to Him through the gospel to "observe all things whatsoever I have commanded you" (Matthew 28:20).

Tolerating Calvin's Errors

Obviously, "all things" meant that each new disciple made by the original disciples was to make disciples, baptize them, and teach them to do likewise. Every true Christian today is a disciple of a disciple of a disciple all the way back to the original disciples—each one having taught the new disciples that they, too, must observe *all things* Christ commanded the original twelve. Were the twelve commanded to baptize and to minister the Lord's Supper? Then so is every true Christian as a successor of the Apostles!

Here we have proof enough that all believers in Christ are qualified to do whatever the original disciples did, including ministering baptism and the Lord's Supper. Christ's own words effectively destroy the fiction of a special clergy class lording it over a laity. One would think that this "great exegete" could see that fact clearly from the Great Commission, but he didn't. This elementary error was the basis of the popish power Calvin wielded in oppressing the citizens of Geneva.

Worse yet, how could the priests and bishops of the Roman Catholic Church, who were not even saved but believed and taught a false salvation through works and ritual, qualify as the successors to the Apostles? And how could Calvinist ministers, who disagreed so markedly with Rome on the gospel, nevertheless be co-successors, sharing with Roman Catholic clergy this exclusive right to baptize and administer the Eucharist? Calvin's "brilliant exegesis" led him into grave error and contradictions so blatant that one wonders how today's Calvinists can overlook or tolerate them.

Furthermore, Calvin also taught that there was no difference between the baptism practiced by John the Baptist and the baptism Christ commanded His disciples to perform: "I grant that John's was a true baptism, and one and the same with the baptism of Christ...the ministry of John was the very same as that which was afterwards delegated to the apostles."[9] That is so clearly wrong that we need not discuss it. John's baptism "unto repentance" (Matthew 3:11) had nothing to do with the believer's identification with Christ in His death, burial, and resurrection, as is the case with the baptism Christ told His disciples to practice.

The fact that Paul considered John's baptism different and inappropriate for believers in Christ (Acts 19:1–6) is explained away by Calvin with the fantastic idea that these hadn't received John's baptism,[10] even though, in response to Paul's question, "Unto what then were you baptized?", they replied, "Unto John's baptism."

It seems that Calvinists are willing to tolerate a great deal of error taught by John Calvin and still consider him to be one of the greatest exegetes in history. From a careful study of what Calvin taught in his *Institutes*, however, we have a far different opinion.

That Calvin was wrong on so many other points ought to ease the pain of having to admit that perhaps he was also wrong on TULIP. Yet the high regard in which Calvin is held apparently prevents this simple admission of serious error on his part.

1. Roland Bainton, *Michel Servet, hérétique et martyr* (Geneva: Droz, 1953), 152-153; letter of February 26, 1533, now lost.

2. John Calvin, *Institutes of the Christian Religion*, trans. Henry Beveridge (Grand Rapids, MI: Wm B. Eerdmans Publishing Co., 1998 ed.), IV: xvi, 4.

3. Ibid., xv, 22; xvi, 3, 4, 8, 10, 17-32.

4. *New Geneva Study Bible*, 38.

5. T.A. McMahon, in an unrecorded interview.

6. Calvin, *Institutes*, IV: xvi, 4.

7. Ibid., xv, 16–17.

8. Ibid., 20.

9. Ibid., 18.

10. Ibid.

A Final Word

MY HEART HAS BEEN BROKEN by Calvinism's misrepresentation of the God of the Bible, whom I love with all my heart, and for the excuse this has given atheists not to believe in Him. My sincere and earnest desire in writing this book has been to defend God's character against the libel that denies His love for all and insists that He does not make salvation available to all because He does not want all to be saved. It is my prayer that readers will recognize that Christian authors and leaders, ancient or modern and no matter how well respected, are all fallible and that God's Word is our only authority.

God's Word declares that the gospel, which is "the power of God unto salvation to *every one that believeth*" (Romans 1: 16), is "good tidings of great joy," not just to certain elect, but "to *all* people" (Luke 2:10). Sadly, the insistence that only a select group have been elected to salvation is *not* "good tidings of great joy to all people"! How can such a doctrine be biblical?

It is my prayer that Calvinist readers who may have gotten this far have been fully persuaded to misrepresent no longer the God of love as having predestinated multitudes to eternal doom while withholding from them any opportunity to understand and believe the gospel. How many unbelievers have rejected God because of this deplorable distortion we do not know—but may that excuse be denied every reader from this time forth! And may believers, in confidence that the gospel is indeed glad tidings for *all* people, take God's good news to the whole world!

—*Dave Hunt*

ABOUT THE BEREAN CALL

***The Berean Call (TBC) is a non-denominational,
tax-exempt organization which exists to:***

ALERT believers in Christ to unbiblical teachings and practices
impacting the church

EXHORT believers to give greater heed to biblical discernment and
truth regarding teachings and practices being currently promoted
in the church

SUPPLY believers with teaching, information, and materials
which will encourage the love of God's truth, and assist in the
development of biblical discernment

MOBILIZE believers in Christ to action in obedience to the
scriptural command to "earnestly contend for the faith" (Jude 3)

IMPACT the church of Jesus Christ with the necessity for trusting
the Scriptures as the only rule for faith, practice, and a life
pleasing to God

*A free monthly newsletter, THE BEREAN CALL, may be received
by sending a request to: PO Box 7019, Bend, OR 97708; or by calling*

1-800-937-6638

*To register for free email updates, to access our digital archives, and to
order a variety of additional resource materials online, visit us at:*

www.thebereancall.org

Made in United States
Troutdale, OR
10/19/2024

23930117R00108